THIS BOOK IS DEDICATED
TO GOD,
CHRIST JESUS AND
THE FAITHFUL APOSTLES!

PROMISED
SAVED
BUT
ONLY
DECEIVED

**Learn about the only way you can obtain
CHRIST JESUS' SALVATION.**
Never let anybody rip you off your faith!

BE
DELIVERED

By
O.C. NOAH

TRAFFORD

• Canada • UK • Ireland • USA •

Note for Librarians: A cataloguing record for this book is available from Library
and Archives Canada at www.collectionscanada.ca/amicus/index-e.html
ISBN 1-4120-7767-2

*Printed in Victoria, BC, Canada. Printed on paper with minimum
30% recycled fibre.*
*Trafford's print shop runs on "green energy" from solar, wind and other
environmentally-friendly power sources.*

Offices in Canada, USA, Ireland and UK
This book was published *on-demand* in cooperation with Trafford Publishing.
On-demand publishing is a unique process and service of making a book
available for retail sale to the public taking advantage of on-demand
manufacturing and Internet marketing. On-demand publishing includes
promotions, retail sales, manufacturing, order fulfilment, accounting and
collecting royalties on behalf of the author.

Book sales for North America and international:
Trafford Publishing, 6E–2333 Government St.,
Victoria, BC v8t 4p4 CANADA
phone 250 383 6864 (toll-free 1 888 232 4444)
fax 250 383 6804; email to orders@trafford.com
Book sales in Europe:
Trafford Publishing (uk) Limited, 9 Park End Street, 2nd Floor
Oxford, UK oxi 1hh UNITED KINGDOM
phone 44 (0)1865 722 113 (local rate 0845 230 9601)
facsimile 44 (0)1865 722 868; info.uk@trafford.com
Order online at:
trafford.com/05-2664

10 9 8 7 6 5 4 3

TABLE OF CONTENTS

OPEN LETTER FROM THE AUTHOR

Dearly beloved, Reader,

You need SALVATION in order to enjoy abundant life on earth and at the end inherit everlasting life. This knowledge about the true salvation must be communicated to you and every other creature according to the commandment of our Lord Jesus Christ.

Unfortunately, there are very many teachings that contravene the TRUTH, which in turn endanger the SALVATION of hearers! However, you can avail yourself of this golden opportunity of freedom by knowing the TRUTH. One must search diligently to be sure he finds the truth because ignorance of the law is no excuse for lawlessness. We do realize that we are indebted to you and the rest of wide world, the duty of evangelizing this TRUTH.

After reading this book make sure you pass it on to a friend, neighbor or just someone else; in doing so you are helping to push the gospel, indirectly; you are also doing the work of God and as a worker in the vineyard you will certainly receive your reward at the fullness of time.

Dearly beloved, do not just do anything you want to with your life because you are writing your own Bible, today!

Do you know that the Bible is a historical record of people who have lived on this planet: some were righteous, some unrighteous, others were wicked and many lived arrogantly. All cases were carefully put together and compiled, for just you and me? Take time to put together the history of your past, so you can save yourself the dangers of making serious mistakes into the future. I have taken time to put down a brief story of my bible that you may truly understand what I mean – THE TESTIMONY OF THE AUTHOR.

If you are a minister of the gospel, we are very willing to help you write the bible of your ministry that you may not be disappointed on the last day. You are very free to operate the doctrine of truth as you read in this book and you may contact us for assistance if you like. On your demand, we shall take time to expound more on the teaching and may get into other vital issues concerning doctrinal matters - if you want us to. We are doing all these because we strongly believe the Word of God to be true to the later. We believe that many will end up in hell fire because they held doctrines of error, which is why we would like to help with the little revelation we have received from the LORD.

I strongly believe that we have had too many denominations and proliferation is another very powerful weapon of Satan against the true church therefore, I am advocating for volunteers who are willing to do the work of God outside denominational umbrella. You don't need circular education to get into this wonderful world-tomorrow; we can help you establish this truth and help spread the good news. If you are willing, contact us today and we will teach you how you can save yourself from the pollution of today and begin to worship God in the way God wants. Again, I will like to re-emphasis this that you need not to be a pastor or one with some seminarian education before you can qualify for this because God is back again like in the days of the early apostles who were common fishermen and never went to school but yet were used mightily by God.

Don't forget that we read of Paul and Peter; excited with the Acts of the apostles and certainly our ministry today must be read as a historical piece sometime in the future and if not in this life maybe in the world to come – for our God loves so much keeping historical records.

Beloved do you realize that God, as the first HISTO-RIAN, has been very careful with those whom He called because He will want such people to always keep historical records of events in their life as a reference into the future. The word of God is more of practical than just a theoretical piece.

May God be with you and empower you as you willingly yield to writing your bible today.

O.C.Noah.

PREFACE

As a part of this critical assignment of rediscovering the truth that has been hidden for years now, you are going to read the most misunderstood doctrine of truth presented with every disgusting detail. You need to be well prepared as to travel on this expedition by having all your study materials intact.

You will be excited to know that God is still what He was in the time past when He saved Daniel from the lion's den; gave victory to the boy David over Goliath and performed wonders to the people who trusted in Him. Most importantly you will learn of an account where the doctrine of salvation was practiced and the result.

The book briefly relates to you of what it is like to be persecuted for the gospel of truth in the day called today without one avenging. It goes on to encourage and also equip you with the knowledge that the truth is not an easy go and if you will believe – there must be a little cross of yours, which you must carry as you follow Christ Jesus.

To make reading very convenient for you and to help your concentration, the book has been divided into two sections. SECTION A dwells on the doctrine of SALVA-TION; it is subdivided into seven inspiring chapters with a concluding part that would always remind you of the key points as to empower you, the reader; it has biblical quotations, no one can contest. The B SECTION is simply a true testimony; you may wish to verify if you want to. You may start from the first section and proceed to the second or you may go to the B section first and return later to A – it is just a matter of your choice.

If you have been pre-ordained, elected and predestined to eternal life we believe that as you read this book, the LORD certainly shall open your heart and give you understanding. Remember that the level of the understanding of any concept could be ascertained by the kind of questions the individual will eventually ask after a teaching. Feel free to ask your questions and may God guard and guide you in the name of Jesus Christ. Amen!

If you accept the message and wish to be initiated into the Lord Jesus Christ in the way you have read and ready to yield to the wholesome truth, we are also ready, very willing and prepared to assist you in the initiation and also to help direct you the more in the issue concerning the entire doctrine of truth.

To contact us, look at the last inside page of this book to get our full address and telephone number.

SECTION A

CHAPTER 1

THE DEAREST PRICE

Imagine you have a bag full of gold and silver and suddenly you see some men point gun on you and there is no way you can defend yourself: *"Your money or your life?"* They thundered! What would you do? A wise man would let go his money for his life. Husbands, how would you feel if before your eyes your wife and children are to be murdered? Would you prefer to die for your family's sake? Or would you just fold your hands and watch the enemy? You have a friend that means so much to you and coincidentally you two look alike. Your friend was found guilty of a capital offense and would be executed publicly at a future date. From detention your very good friend escaped to unknown destination; since you resemble your friend in missed identity you are caught by the police. How would you react and what would you do? Will you simply follow like a sheep led to the slaughter, or would you aid the police to fish out the run-away since you know every of his hideouts? We are going to read how a single individual had gone a long way to positively affect these life questions.

It is an established fact confirmable by historical records that more than ninety nine percent of humanity would prefer to loose all that they have only to stay alive and well. Just an infinitesimal few would rather die for their money, family or friend. The Bible explains this with the lives of the great men of history. Abraham for example was a great man of his time, devoted to serve God but a time came for him to choose to loose his beautiful wife or die to let her live on. When famine struck the land that necessitated that father Abraham would leave the place he was living to go into a region dominated by ungodly people and knowing that his wife was very beautiful and what could happen to a man who would not let go he consulted with the wife and they two agreed to diplomatically pretend to be unmarried. Such action if it were not that God intervened could have meant the breaking apart of the lovely family of Abraham but in all; they would rather live at the expense of the marriage relationship than to be consumed by famine. Gen.12: 10-13. Abraham preferred to let go his wife than to die for his wife.

In the case of Job, while the wife turned into an agent of Satan, because of fear, everything that Job had, including children, Satan, the enemy, consumed; even the skin of Job became leprous. God valued only one thing differently with express commandment to its regard. But a righteous man ought not to suffer and God's testimony can never be wrong, for Job was truly doing his best to live righteously and God was very proud of Job that HE had to challenge the devil concerning this faithful servant but Satan took advantage of God's testimony to accuse Job of conditional obedience. The LORD still was very confident in Job and what a great news and joy of victory that the man Job did not disappoint God, all to the shame of the devil. The devil had power over every thing that was belonging to Job but was not allowed by God to touch the life of Job. The devil perhaps refused touching the wife of Job maybe because she already had gone into partnership with Satan to see a way the man Job could be induced into blaspheming against God. Job 2:3-6. The life of Job was most expensively regarded and there was nothing more important.

Man can make sacrifices with what he has even to the point of giving out wife and children in order to safe-guard his own life. It is most unusual for the man to will-ingly sacrifice his life for any reason whatsoever. Only in rare cases has history recorded of men who gave their lives to save other things belonging to them.

Maybe the reason why men would prefer to live at the expense of those things belonging to them is that their wealth is secure while they are alive and becomes vulner-able after they die. For no man can be able to control and supervise what belongs to him after his demise. It takes extreme commitment and sometimes-deep spirituality for man to grudgingly sacrifice his own life for some minor purposes.

The dearest price in the context of our study could be defined as those exceptional sacrifices in which case the one sacrificing uses his very best and only possession to give in order to redeem an entangled and loveable entity. However, it may be easy for a person to give up personal belongings in other to save a loved one but issue becomes very difficult when ransom is only for the price of ones life – no man can do this for just his friends but Christ did it; not just only for his friends but also for his enemies. John 15:13, Rom. 5:8.

Our Lord Jesus Christ died to save us, the church, which represent his friends and as well as his enemies which is represented by the rest of the world that know not God.

Tracing the origin of paying the dearest price could mean going very far into eternity past because every doctrine and teachings that is commanded by God was first of all demonstrated by the same LORD; for man to emulate. God wanted to teach us how to truly love, that HE sacrificed HIS only Son that we, who has been dead in sin and unrighteousness may have life through Him. We did not contribute to this miracle or did we in any way impress God but out of sincere and unconditional mercy, Christ Jesus was sent by the FATHER to be a payment for our sins. God did all of this to set example which we must follow. 1 John 4:9-11.

Sometime in eternity past there did exist only the ETERNAL FATHER like an unmarried young man. The POWER (Holy Spirit), including LOGOS (The Word of God) was all inside the ETERNAL FATHER. The ETERNAL at a point decided to expand HIS family and by HIS infinite POWER commanded HIS WORD to become an independent Spirit Being like the FATHER; the Firstborn of creation. The Son of God is the radiance of God's glory and wherever the FATHER may not be able to go because of HIS uncompromising GLORY, HE sends HIS Son to represent HIM. Imagine how the Son has been lifted up by the FATHER in the entire Kingdom of GOD; for no spirit or angel has received at any time the pronouncement of adoption by the FATHER and none had GOD at any time given the privilege of sharing HIS worship save the Son. Heb. 1:3, 5 & 6.

By the WORD of GOD who has now become like GOD; every other creation came into existence!

The Son was the authority of the ETERNAL FA-

THER in creating things, which also was staked for the reason of expanding more the Divine family, otherwise known as mankind. After the Son of GOD, the second most glorified creature is man. Every other creature were made for the enjoyment of the man and though the devil and his fallen angels are jealous of man, the LORD who made him has so much lavished His love on man that the kingdom of darkness can not overcome him. John 1:1-5.

The first adventure of the ETERNAL expanding HIS family empire was very successful that the ETERNAL FATHER, impressed by the activities of HIS WORD whom HE made to exist independently, promoted LOGOS to become HIS SON. The joy of the success of the first adventure yielded to the second, where man was involved. However, the man unlike LOGOS failed the test and was corrupted by Satan the devil. Since the ETERNAL FATHER already loved man, there was a need to rescue the man from the hands of Satan and somebody must be willing to offer himself as to accomplish the mission. Great and powerful arch angels like Michael and Raphael fought many unsuccessful wars against Satan and his fallen angels in the bid of rescuing man and when it became evident that mission was impossible the ETERNAL FATHER was burdened. Who again will be able to go at this crucial time? Was a question that brought every activity in the KINGDOM of GOD to a stand still! Great surprise shook the entire KINGDOM as the Son of God abdicated his Royal seat as to go and save man to the glory of the FATHER. Is. 6:8.

For the sake of love, LOGOS offered Himself as a redeeming sacrifice to rescue man from the hands of Satan. Jesus Christ, who was God, offered Himself as a sacrifice in demonstration of His love for mankind and to please the ETERNAL FATHER; setting example for the doctrine and tradition of paying the dearest price, which man MUST emulate. The effectiveness of paying the dearest price is on the willingness of the mind to act without compulsion of any kind only to please God. Our Lord Jesus Christ was not forced to go and pay the price of the salvation of man but He took the challenge upon Himself and for this reason the FATHER will always love Him. We should not wait until our sister/brother come to us begging for alms or hold-on until we are pushed before realizing the need for the preaching of the gospel but the more willing we are to do the will and purpose of GOD, the deeper HE loves us. We have been given the commandment to love and therefore we need not to wait until necessity is laid on us. John 10:17, 18.

No wonder the divine rule will always stand and God's word, immutable!

Delivering the message of paying the dearest price to us, the church today, our Lord Jesus Christ, made very explicit expressions. Have you ever stopped to give taught about what it is by denying your own self and taking your cross: it means that you cannot be able to enter into the Kingdom of God when you are selfish, for no arrogant man can be able to follow after Jesus Christ with his own little cross. Therefore, we must be selfless and disciplined in mind as to have enough obedience in our system which will give us the golden opportunity of becoming true disciples of Jesus Christ. In any battle the cowardice are the very first that die in the field of war because they are always reluctant to make quick decisions as to immediately take dangerous adventures and since successes at war are seriously regulated by time, the fearful die many times but the brave will tell the story what happened in the battle field. Luke 9:23, 24. To be sure the disciples did not consider this teaching as a proverbial statement our Lord went further to emphasize that in order to come closer to God, man must give up his pride; for example, your neighbors that used to know you as a wicked person or your family that has not known peace should rejoice when you have truly encountered Christ Jesus. Everything that blow up your mind and made you in the time past to be cruel and unapproachable must be changed to uplift those you humbled in time past as evidence of your salvation miracle. Some use their wealth to intimidate and humble those under them; when people like that come to the faith, they should show the evidence of their new birth by changing, using their resources this time to help the weak and heal the wounds they had inflicted in time past. Matt. 19:21. Of course Jesus was telling us that all bridges behind us must be burnt to avoid any one retreating from the Kingdom race. This perfecting law was not specially presented in order to ward off the rich young man but was the fulfillment of the tradition of Offerings and Sacrifices as were held according to the law in the Old Testament. At the fullness of time this doctrine was revealed to the church after they had received the Holy Spirit and those who desired to be made perfect, practiced the doctrine. What will it look like to come to a family where there are no more needy persons because those who have valuable properties like lands and houses; sold them and distributed the proceeds to those that were of low estate. What preacher who has been called by God will not do the work of God more gladly and ever-praising God when he realizes that the wife and children would not lack the basic necessities of life. For both small and great, this is one of the greatest miracles that have ever happened to the church of God in Christ Jesus. And what an understanding that a descendant from the tribe of Levi who could have been busy trying to recover his former rights in priesthood according to the law but instead was the first to give as to demonstrate this doctrine. Acts 4:34-37. This goes further to re-enforce the fact that the priesthood was shifted from the tribe of Levi to the lineage of the king David and with the change a corresponding approach and amending of the law attached to priesthood also took effect. Heb. 7:11- 20.

It is very unfortunate that over the years we have

misconstrued the doctrine of the dearest price. It is also true that many do acknowledge that, *'Giving time is blessing time'* however, very many of us do not understand that the way and manner that we exercise the doctrine of giving has so much bearing on our salvation. After all, we can only enter into the Kingdom of God when we have become like God in every aspect including our giving habit. How justified can we be to God and to our ambition to become like God when we treat the things of God like the unbelievers of old? Before we practice any doctrine, it is very important to be well informed of all the aspects because half-truth is more dangerous than wholesome lie. For example the doctrine of paying the dearest price requires that a brother or sister sells his/her belonging and the full price he/she lays to the feet of the apostles and no part of the price should be taken away. Just as it was in the days of old where a life cattle is brought to the LORD for sacrifice and the giver moves away without any part of what he had brought. The incident of Ananias and Saphira happened in the new testament, as a warning to every one of us using the doctrine of the LORD carelessly – it is not only identifying the doctrine but we must practice it exactly and in accordance to the commandment of our Lord Jesus Christ. If doing the doctrine wrongly would amount to capital punishment as in the case of Ananias and Saphirah then judge for yourself what it will be for people who have chosen to celebrate pagan feasts like Christmas and Easter all in the name of the LORD - shall not the Most High do much more to them than He did to Ananias and Saphirah? Acts 5:1-10.

Though we are all beggars before the Almighty God who is the Owner of all things, yet our LORD did not give unto us as beggarly as we are but instead the Most High offered His best to save poor sinners like you and me. If God who is the GREATEST has favored man with so great an honor, shall any be justified when he/she gives to God like a beggar down the street? First and foremost we should realize that we all are priests and kings to God by the virtue of the new covenant in Christ Jesus and all our devotions and service are sacrifices and offerings to God and must be rendered accordingly. We must be more careful with our lives because God has chosen us and made us priests in the ROYAL ORDER, a nation called to the HOLINESS OF JEHOVAH GOD. We would not behave like the world where we are, but as strangers we should be practicing and demonstrate the uniqueness of life in accordance to the commandments of the world tomorrow. 1 Peter 2:9. It is upon us, the church, that the prophesies of Malachi are seriously pointing to, like never before. If we realize truly that we are a royal priesthood unto the LORD then we ought to show some honor to the High Priest of our calling and also give glory to the FATHER ALMIGHTY at least comparable to the devotion we give to our boss in our places of work, but we don't! The LORD is pointing accusing fingers directly to those that have been called and ordained unto glory because they show nonchalant attitude to the things belonging to God. For our worship unto God include; the righteousness we exhibit on our every day life, the devotions we give for the things of God and the sacrifices we make to the preaching of the gospel. It is a sin against God and the church for a brother/sister who have been blessed by God to watch the gospel suffer for none availability of financial resources when such could help the LORD. If the state will always tax their citizens according to the level of their income and expenditure and a person may be prosecuted by law if such is found maneuvering tax; shall not the Most High judge us even more how we lavish the gift of wealth He has blessed us with, spending our money on the pleasures of this life more than the things of God. The much you give to the things of God, if you present it to the governor of your state or even to our dear President will he be able to grant you more favor? But we are talking about the God who is the maker of both the President and those whom that are governed. Mal. 1:6-8.

If we must be perfected in our calling we must be willing and prepared to give exactly as our God; that is the assurance of our salvation. On the other hand, to keep the church away from the blood guilt of the innocent, those that handle the finances of the church must do so with every honesty and fear of God knowing that their ministry might influence the peace of the church and affect the salvation of many.

God is not requiring from you and me alms because HE is not poor but remains the SOVERIGN LORD: there is nothing you can give unto God that is worth more than the things you already have received from HIM. You must give to the LORD all that you have to be able to come to the corridors of the ALMIGHTY – you start with your life and then demonstrate the same in the works of your hands. The LORD will have us to know that it is not impossible for Him to throw money from heaven so that the gospel could be preached or command blessings from the wild forest so that the hungry could be feed but God have kept a judgment for you and for me what we do with the wealth of this life and the ministry we have received. The Most High would always give His wealth to somebody or some people to pass on to others just as He also has ordained some particular people to preach the gospel – each and everyone of us shall appear before the judgment seat of Christ and give account on how we utilized the recourses of our calling. Rom. 14:12.

Let me say emphatically that God would abhor your wealth when you refuse to give your own soul, thinking that you can earn salvation through your money or gifts because giving God your money is one thing but yielding to the Almighty is the greatest. That does not mean that the church cannot accept gifts from outside the body or to ask for some favors if the need arises; yet, more concentration must be placed on the saving of the soul and not on the acquisition of material wealth. The time was fully come that our Lord Jesus Christ will triumphantly enter Jerusalem to fulfill a very important aspect of prophesy: neither Peter nor the rest apostles were possessors of colt but yet the Master must enter Jerusalem riding on a colt. Luke 19:30, 31. Our Lord, Jesus Christ used this circumstance to warn the church that where for any reason they default to provide for the Ministry He has the power to command people from the outside to contribute as to be sure the church marches on.

So my brothers and sisters be prepared to give the greatest gift unto GOD by yielding yourself to the calling into the one true Body of Christ Jesus – don't just give GOD alms meant for the poor, He needs your life and soul.

CHAPTER 2

THE ORIGIN OF MAN

A good number of people confessing Christ Jesus as their personal Lord and Savior will miss the Kingdom of Heaven; not because they committed adultery and/or other related offenses but because they held doctrines of error. Many will also be disappointed in the last day because of their unwillingness to come to the full knowledge of whom the Lord Jesus Christ really is. Not knowing what the true faith is and trusting in some other things will surely question the salvation of many into hell. Worst, a great number of believers would wander irreparably because they are unable to find their names in the lamb's book of life. Reason? They were not buried with Christ according to the doctrine.

The church of the living God brings to you the revealed truth emphasizing that there is only one true body of Christ Jesus and this one body is controlled by the one Spirit or GOD which gives them one hope because they are united to the one LORD, they have only one doctrinal faith, having received the baptism into Christ Jesus which also has adopted them into the family of the one God and FATHER of all, who is the Beginning and the End, the Creator and Maker of all things. Ephs. 4:4-6. This gives us the idea that there could be many bodies, yet there is one body; different hopes, yet there is one hope; many lords yet there is only one LORD; diverse faith yet there is only one true faith; baptisms, yet one baptism; many gods and fathers, yet there is the one true GOD and FATHER of us all. No matter the level of spiritual achievement of any individual/s or the consciousness of holiness, as long as such person/s hold/s this/these in error, it is impossible for such to inherit the promise of everlasting life.

We are very much aware that many people today do antagonize and persecute the truth because they lack the knowledge and understanding just as it was with Saul, who later became Paul. The Church of Jesus Christ is charged with the obligation to presenting to you the TRUTH without compromise; that whereas churches exist, yet we should be aware that there is only one TRUE CHURCH.

In this our short study of God's unity plan, we shall be looking into the revealed truth about SALVATION; extracting from scriptures pure facts about this doctrinal issue, how it was received and how it should be practiced.

Man is a unique creature and unlike other creatures, man did not come into existence by the simple WORD command but through a careful and meticulous approach by God. With other creatures, God spoke them into existence, which perhaps could be further interpreted that it was

28

the WORD of GOD that made these creatures. But when it came to the sixth day of creation, towards the evening, the ETERNAL in partnership with the SON condescended low to carefully pick dust from the earth with which THEY *builded* the man. To create man was a task that needed the representation of the two persons in the GODHEAD; therefore, a call came from the FATHER employing the company of the SON. Gen. 1:26.

That the FATHER employed the company of HIS SON is a great mystery rooted in the LOVE of God unto us (mankind). When the man was made: the FATHER was tangibly present with the SON and they carefully selected the dust elements. The touching of the dust by the DIVINE automatically quickened matter; making the molded dustman to have the influence of God otherwise known as the *spirit of man* or *conscience*. The spirit of man or conscience is a common gift of God to all mankind, it does not discriminate but both the righteous and the unrighteous has conscience and no man can run away from his conscience. It is this conscience that makes some people feel guilt to the extreme of committing suicide, it is also the conscience that make it possible for man to receive repentance – it is the tape recorder of God in the soul of man and it will be our conscience that will judge us on the last day. Gen. 2:7. If your conscience does not condemn you, you are justified but where it does gently reprimand you, you are condemned already. To be sure man will not cheat his conscience, the GODHEAD performed a wonderful most fulfilling miracle in the favor of man by imparting the Divine nature into the man. Our Lord Jesus Christ revealed this Divine nature to us as the 'HOLY SPIRIT'.

With the breath of life from God into Adam, the man was fully equipped with power to live right. The creation of the woman was an extension of man's empire, which became a testing instrument to ascertain how obedient the

29

man could be unto God if he enters into his estate. Man, who was equipped with the power and wisdom to lead however, lost his glory because he would prefer pleasing his wife than God. The consequences of Adam's disobedience and the continuity of transgressions brought about the severing of the Holy Spirit of God away from man which is the fulfillment of the WORD of GOD; for God already had spoken about death in a way man was unable to comprehend - this is spiritual death. Gen. 6:3. Any person living in this planet earth without the indwelling of the Spirit of God is dead while he/she still lives in the flesh because the one is cut off with communication from God and behaves the way he/she likes and bears curse. The ETERNAL withdrew HIS Holy Spirit from the man and his seed and since the Spirit, is holy, cannot abide in unholy vessel therefore, the man who has been banished from paradise, went his way empty and vulnerable which the devil in turn took advantage of. Another thing very significant of the banishment of man is that it is impossible for the man to have the indwelling of the Divine nature away from Paradise, in the same way it is impossible for any man to have the true Holy Spirit of God without first identifying himself with the doctrine of truth and to belong to the true church.

The devil saw the banishment of man as his greatest opportunity and consulting with man against God, Satan encouraged the man to be enemy of God. With man entering into covenant with Satan, man-God relationship was severed. After the sin of Adam, man was never again considered as a *living soul*; however, since man's conscience came by the touching of God and whereas man has remained stable at least by his physical composure therefore, the *spirit of the man* or his *conscience* has remained with the man to date leaving the man only, a simple *soul*. It is terrific what man can do when he is in his right mood with his conscience but that is not enough to make the man truly the master of creation which he was originally ordained.

By composition man could be described in two loca-
tions namely: when man was originally created and after
man lost his position. In the original creation of man, the
man is composed of three elements: the *dust*, the *spirit of
man* or *conscience* and then the *loaned spirit from God*. After the man lost his position as the image and likeness of
God, the man was left with a *residual*, composed of only the
dust and the *conscience*, without the *empowering Spirit*.

Adam and Eve were the parents of the world and by
the visitation of iniquity of parents unto their children; the
descendants were placed under hereditary curse. It has been
with man from the day he was made that children born into
the family are automatically inheritors of all that belong to
their parents, the good and the bad. No inheritor will have to
take his/her possession without accepting the liabilities and
responsibilities attached. Mankind being descendants of
Adam and Eve had no choice than to accept the sin already
in the family, face death and become inventors of wickedness. Rom. 5:12. Mankind did not become sinners because
of the act of sin but because we were born as inheritors of
the first Adam – who became sin from disobedience. The
commandment and laws of God did not exist in the days
of old Adam and wife, Eve, since it was only man and wife
therefore there were no need to say things like; *'you should
not look lustfully on a woman or you should not think of
taking your neighbor's wife'*.   Adam was judged according
to the foundation of God's righteousness rooted in simple
obedience.

After Adam and Eve, the parents of mankind, many
have risen with the burden of bringing man back to his lost
glory. Judges, kings, prophets and so on have ventured un-
successfully in bringing man back to God. Since these ad-
venturers were mortals and descendants of Adam therefore,
the seed of error was also in them, making them unable to
deliver. People like Moses, Jeremiah, and Isaiah, including

31

great men of God of our time undoubtedly received some messages from God, which they exaggerated, underestimated or misrepresented. Could you imagine how the Pharisees and Sadducees came smartly hoping to trap the LORD with their question in reference to the interpretation of marriage as was given to them by their great lawgiver, Moses. But why was Moses so weak to declare the full consul of God without fear or favor and instead of the people to have the compassion and love understanding they preferred to follow the ways of Moses rather than to obey God. Every Israelite has special love and honor to the man Moses not for any other reason but because the man was/is an aide in the devil's compromising program. With Moses the average Israelite is covered and the aims and aspirations of the people is gravely considered to the expense of the true laws of mercy and liberty. Mark 10: 2-9.

Sentiments and pressures of life made messengers of God not to present God's messages raw to the people and so their messages became ineffective. All the prophets that spoke in time past, the priests that handled the things in the Temple, including each and every elder that has risen and will rise in the future; who will not declare the Word of God, raw as he has received it, has a single adjective which they are qualified with in the spiritual – they are thieves. Have you ever considered the devastating effects of the laws of Moses on the worship of God today and how people have in the same vein attached themselves more to the teachings of elders than the undiluted Word of God, stealing away the hearts and minds of men over to ceremonial and ritual worship than equity and righteousness. People are made to believe the lie; answering altar call, confessing their sins before a preacher and led to Christ by repeating some words and afterwards, they get their bible and identify themselves with one living churches around having been pronounced saved – not minding the doctrine. 2 John 1:9.

True prophecies of old were pointing to one thing: revealing a particular personality, however, those who research into them without the Spirit empowerment can hardly realize that Christ Jesus is the overall fulfillment. The wrong knowledge of the Israelites about God took the nation of God to assume that they were upholding a religion just like the nations around them. Israel will always like to have some objects of worship but when the LORD blocked every of their attempts to make for themselves idols and objects of worship they then decided to take Moses to be their living idol. When Moses was taken away from their sight and buried in an unknown place, they sort diligently for the body of Moses, not because they would like to mourn for Moses and give him a befitting burial but they wanted a place where they would completely establish their idol worship in the name of Moses. The priests, prophets and kings of Israel did not come to the full knowledge of God and understanding of the life to come because while GOD was preparing to reveal the Messiah, they compared the ALMIGHTY with heathen gods just as some confessing believers have today chosen Christian religion alter than Christ-life. John 5:39. Many prophets who received the revelation of Christ Jesus' personality desired so strongly to witness the manifestation but were not privileged but for the few who beheld it, greatest joy overtook them. Simon, the high priest who rose in the days when the child Jesus was born saw through the revelations of God that the birth of the Messiah was at hand and therefore refused to die pleading with the ALMIGHTY to preserve his life as to witness this Great Miracle. Great priests, prophets and kings of God who lived before Simon also saw concerning the coming Messiah and waited in vain but were not opportune to witness the manifestation. After Simon saw the miracle he then yielded to God to bring him home to rest because according to him, he has seen God's salvation. From the encounter of Simon with the child Jesus we can vividly deduct that the salvation of God unto us is not the religion Christianity or even the Mosaic concept rather, it is the revelation of a particular personality. It there means that we are saved when we are able to practice and live our life exactly as with the man Jesus Christ. The prophet also remarked that our LORD would be the light that will brighten the path of the Gentiles as to be integrated into the one nation of God – ISRAEL. Luke 2:28-32.

Our God is a meticulous God that would always balance and perfect every program that HE has started and at the same time HE makes every man and woman inexcusable. For when Simon had finished speaking and prophesying concerning our LORD, it did not stop at that because the salvation God had brought, will favor both man and woman therefore a prepared vessel, a prophetess, Anna, came to the scene and spoke as she was led by the Spirit of God to the hearing of all the people that were there. So if you are waiting for the redemption of your family, tribe or nation you cannot get salvation from any other person or thing alter than our Lord Jesus Christ. On the other hand, God would want the women to be very much encouraged and realize that God's salvation is for them also just as it is for the men, at least by the representation of Anna, the prophetess. Luke 2:36-38.

The prophets of old did not stop in merely prophesying about the coming Messiah rather, they extended their vision into the attitude and way of life of the coming Christ. God never hid anything concerning Christ away from His servants, the prophets: the way the Messiah would live and the kind and manner of death he would die were foretold and all came to pass; which goes to authenticate the truth of Christ Jesus' Divine incarnation.

CHAPTER 3

WHEN TOUCHED BY GOD!

The earth has existed from ages and the phenomena of total eradication of life has occurred and reoccurred at different times. It wasn't that God took pleasure in destroying the works of HIS hands but, the man, whom the LORD made to be the governor of creation, instead of ruling and leading creation joined forces with Satan and his emissaries to invent and develop wickedness at every second, minute and hour of his life. Imagine how much the decay became of concern with God that the God who cannot repent now saw regret in the creation of man. When an enemy takes over a very important work of art and hold some citizens hostage and it becomes very clear that he would never give up the possession of the area neither release those he has held hostage and where the presence of the terrorist and his occupation is a potential threat, the only solution will be to destroy both the terrorist, the great work of art and even the hostages. The alliance of man and devil became a potential threat to the Kingdom and Personality of God that the only alternative was a complete eradication of man's civilization. But it has been the tradition of the LORD not to destroy the righteous with the wicked and when the man Noah rose in those days, the LORD also honored him with salvation as a reward of his obedience and righteousness. Gen. 6:8. Whenever God decided destroying life completely, there has always been a remnant that was left. The survivors in the delude of Noah for example were saved by their faith and obedience to the water of the Word which made them to engage in the blood-pains of building the ark according to the commandment of God. It is not just hearing God that matters but the most important is to listen and obey the LORD, for Noah had the choice of disregarding the revelations of God. Certainly, God did not come down physically to approach Noah but rather he must have received some revelations, maybe some kind of a dream, vision or audible voice, which others may also encounter and take no notice of. It takes faith for a man to use his personal resources to invest into a program, which is unpopular and has no direct economic gain. We sometimes have dreams and some of us may consider such as fantasies while others like Noah would not take it as an ordinary nightmare and when he was made to understand that a greater power was coming against man and the entire creation he simply desired to pay any price that maybe required so as to be favored, himself and his family, if it were possible. Gen. 6:13, 14, 17& 18.

Before any people or person can experience salvation from God, there must first be the touching of the individual by the supreme power, the Almighty FATHER. It is the ETERNAL FATHER, HIM alone, has the keys to open the hearts of men. The eight that were saved from the delude received their salvation because they were first touched by the ETERNAL FATHER who empowered them with faith as to believe the word of God. Their faith gave them power to work obediently and untiringly unto the finishing of the ark. There were no restriction orders against any that lived in the days of Noah rather, the invitation was opened to all and sundry and the LORD was patient enough to endure humanity at that time for very long time until when every other person tuned down the offer of God's salvation, Noah and his family embraced it and became the only survivors of the delude. 1 Pet. 3:20.

The children of Israel in Egypt received some express commandments from God that they strictly obeyed and with the blood on the lintel, salvation came to the children of God with automatic condemnation upon all Egyptians. THE CHILDREN OF ISRAEL WERE SAVED BECAUSE THEY ACTED ACCORDINGLY AFTER GOD ALMIGHTY GAVE THEM THE SPIRIT AS TO BELIEVE THE WATER OF THE WORD OF GOD. When God commanded Moses and instructed him concerning the killing of the lamb and the sprinkling of the blood upon the doorpost what was required of the Israelites was only the work of faith, which needed no investigation – for they need not to be detailed how the killing angel would work. They were even confined to their houses and were forbidden to come out during that miraculous night because God will have to do HIS thing HIS own way. Heb. 11:28.

Coming to the red sea, the children of Israel were confused; not knowing where to follow, again, the Spirit came down and enabled Moses to act to the dividing of the red sea for Israel to walk on dry ground. ISRAEL WAS SAVED BY THE WATER OF THE WORD OF GOD, AND THE SPIRIT POWER, WHICH TOOK THEM THROUGH BAPTISM INTO MOSES. But why again should we be ignorant about the workings of salvation program of God?

And why would our LORD each time HE comes to save HIS people will always choose to do so through some kind of baptism? All the shadows in the past came down to tangible reality when the LORD brought all prophecies into fulfillment and at the same time commanded that the only way we can attain to the grace of GOD is to receive the baptisms that He personally established. The eight in the days of Noah were saved through baptism, and the same baptism destroyed all those that were not inside the ark just as the Israelites also were baptized into Moses while they went through the cloud and the sea, which in turn destroyed Pharaoh and his army. Whenever a person has been baptized and saved by God he/she must experience the joy of partaking in the food of angels and having been hooked to the commonwealth of God, the life which such would live from hence will be of and for the LORD; such will no more be the pilot of his life because the Holy Spirit of God has taken over. 1Cor. 10:1-4. O, what a wonderful mystery, the same water, which the children of Israel passed through and were saved, were the same that consumed the Egyptians. Yes, it was the same gospel that was preached to the entire Jewish state, which converted the twelve apostles and at the same time provoked some other Jews to rebel against their Maker. At this point I must employ you to this prayer; that God may not use you as a vessel that will be dishonored in the house of God, because when it was time that God wanted to glorify HIS Son on earth through death, Judas Iscariot became an instrument of disgrace. Rom. 9:21. After the children of Israel had passed successfully through the red sea, Pharaoh and his army saw the miracle of the sea tearing apart and instead of them to fear and withdraw from pursuing the people of God; they thought they could maneuver somehow. This is a lesson we all must learn as to avoid ourselves taking short cuts when it comes to the dealing of God. Many are living witnesses of the realities of God which the LORD has revealed to them but they seem not to fear and to obey God but would rather wage war against the

LORD and HIS anointed – only to end in the belly of fish. Ex. 14:26, 27.

I wish to emphasize once again that salvation does not occur accidentally but there must be some Divine encounter that would give man, power, touching the conscience in order to open understanding. There would also be the WATERING OF THE WORD, which includes precise instructions that point at some particular things that the man MUST do to obtain the righteousness belonging to God. Unless all these are carefully followed and accomplished, salvation can never come exactly as it is in the mind of God. Do you not know that there are people who are out there watching their weight because they would not like to be disqualified from participating in some tournament; such people skip meals and subject themselves to strenuous exercises just to make sure they come out in flying colors in their various endeavors: shall not the race into the Kingdom of God require some training and sacrifices? Of course there are some sacrifices one must pay and trainings which we must obtain before we maybe counted worthy of entering into the Kingdom of God.1 Cor. 9:25.

Man out of the mechanism of obedience/disobedience yielded himself to Satan the devil and as a result became enemy of God. He was formally a son but turned and become a stranger and allies with Satan, the enemy of God, and all that is of God. Man did not undertake the mission of terror against God consciously rather; he was however manipulated by the devil into behaving badly. Col. 1:21. The devil did not pay any fees for the soul of man, rather, man was held bound by the simple command of interest thereof; the man MUST NEVER be redeemed with perishable things. That salvation is free did not occur accidentally; but man by his personal volition walked unto the devil without any official consultation with God who is the Owner of the soul of man. Whenever the man comes to his rightful mind, all he need is to also walkout from the devil without having to pay back anything. Is. 52:3.

WARNING! Salvation and other gifts from God can never be bought with money or money's worth: those who receive, receive freely, likewise, those that will give MUST give freely. Man was not created to be sick; he was not made to be dieing; the body of man was not for infirmity and the mind of man was not fashioned to accommodate evil spirits therefore, we have the right to life and we would get all these, FREELY, the moment we identify with CHRIST JE-SUS. Matt. 10:8.

On the other hand, to obtain favor and blessings those receiving gifts from God are encouraged to show their appreciations to such goodness. It is morally wrong to obtain free gifts without appreciating the source that has made the provisions available. When we are made to receive gifts that money cannot buy, shall we not be more thankful to God who has liberated us from the devil and given us another opportunity to live a wholesome life? That man is unthankful and unappreciated when he is shown some favors is an attribute of Satan the devil and in fact, it is another way of making man detestable before God as to bringing him back into bondage. Why? The law controlling goodness requires that each good done to one must be returned or reciprocated in equal value and when the greater has favored the lesser then must the lesser pay back with thanksgiving else, the goodness will be retorted spiritually and the lesser will suffer even more severe loss than before. Luke 17:11-19.

Though our Lord Jesus Christ did command that we should not demand payments for spiritual gifts and services that are rendered through us, yet appreciation from the receiver's end go a long way to praise and worship God and to make permanent the miracle. It is true that the Bible did not record that the other nine lepers that were healed lost their miracle after-all, yet, from the statement of our Lord, there must be some difference between the nine who did not come to praise and thank God and the one that came back.

All the time God would always like to test our receiving ability by our giving capability; suggesting that we practice the giving habit in our own little capacity. Our destiny is to be exactly like God and if we would achieve this ambition we must be willing to give and ever ready to share the goodness of God unto us. First and foremost it is not a good omen when we always receive some kind of gift from someone without us having something we could pass on to others. In circumstances where a person becomes a parasite both in mind and in body, such have contacted in the spiritual what I may call incurable poverty syndrome. Acts 20:35.

The more any person is able to obey the law regulating human success and is able to give and keep on giving, then shall the circle of prosperity be completed on the economy of such one, ushering in the manifestation of the miracle which brings in goodness because goodness has been given out. And with more willingness to give, blessings will come like the waves of the sea and before you know it, it will come all over you and overtake you – your shores will be enlarged and your joy shall know no end. For the LORD will surely visit you abundantly in return. Luke 6:38. You shouldn't wait until demand is laid on you to give for the preaching of the gospel or alms for your poor neighbor. But we should also note that any gift that has been grudgingly given has no reward before God but one should first understand this ministry very adequately so that he can gladly and generously give knowing fully well that God is somewhere evaluating and judging our giving habits. Before you give, try very hard to consult and consent with your inner man and let it not be as if you are being persuaded against your will because your arrogance or cheerfulness will also come up on the day you will be judged by God. You that has enough money to selfishly spend, don't you realize that there could also be some other things you may be lacking on which you would certainly have a need for – if no other thing, what about your life? It is possible to get longer life through our healthy giving habits and you are safer when the people whom you have touched their lives through your charity make intercessions to God on your behalf. 2 Cor. 9:5-9.

Do not resist the Spirit of God whenever ministration is laid in your heart to give; that could be the beginning of God's answer to your age long prayer!

CHAPTER 4

RIGHTEOUSNESS OF MAN
&
RIGHTEOUSNESS BELONGING TO GOD

When every effort made to rescue man failed woefully and with the burden of sin telling hard on the children of Adam and Eve, out of love another master plan, which already was drawn from the foundation of the world, came into effect. God's rescue operation took a different dimension and this time God decided to do the most unthinkable through the Holy Spirit. To prove to humanity that the GODHEAD was involved in this unique process of bringing home the already prepared salvation of God unto man, a most unprecedented thing happened; a virgin, who have known no man conceived not by the copulation of man and woman but through the power of the ALMIGHTY GOD. Matt. 1:18. The child that was born of Mary, Jesus, felt like every other man, yet he lived a victoriously, sinless life, establishing a satisfaction that the first Adam was fully equipped by God to lead a righteous life. That our LORD, was God with us, did not make Him any way different from feeling like every other person and just like you and me, our Master had the challenges of the drives in human impulses and temptations did not let Him alone, but in all these experiences, He remained faultless. Heb. 4: 15. Jesus Christ by the righteousness of God which he yielded himself to, became the perfection God was requiring from man and as a consequence, the last Adam. Adam whose marriage with the wife Eve lasted for just a short while also had a brief indwelling of the Holy Spirit of God because of his advent of sin. But Christ Jesus, who is the last Adam, by His unalloyed obedience to the FATHER, received the Holy Spirit of God without measure and therefore has the ability of transforming the lives of men and women, like you and me to the glory of God, whom He will also be joined in wedlock for a time without end. 1 Cor. 15:45.

Throughout the generations of man righteousness has remained a perfect instrument of measuring the conduct of man in his community. To promote righteousness, several laws are made and enforced and all them that obey the laws of the land are regarded as honorable in their various societies. Coming to the relationship between God and man, God is the greatest in one part with the weak man in another part; there is impossibility of association considering the difference in-between. To bridge the gap, the weak man must wear strength through the impartation of the righteousness belonging to God. Alms to the poor; abstinence from fornication/adultery; hospitality; philanthropy and so on are righteousness belonging to the man and such righteousness only improves the physical well being of man and his neighbors. The righteousness belonging to man as named above can never earn man everlasting life.

There is this righteousness belonging to God!

This righteousness of God has no human definition since it comes according to Divine programming. No mortal man can claim pre-knowledge of the righteousness belonging to God but for the elect of God the only readiness in this area is absolute obedience. Take for instance in the righteousness belonging to man, the law stipulates that mortal man has no right whatsoever to take the life of his fellow man. Ex. 20:13. Even when the law has not been given through Moses, God did not take it lightly with Cain who murdered his brother, Abel. Man has no authority whatsoever to take away his own life or the life of his fellow man and because of the offering of human sacrifice; God dispossessed the land of promise from the original inhabitants. But coming to the righteousness of God in the circumstance of Abraham: the LORD first reminded Abraham that HE needed a sacrifice from him but this time not from his sheep, cattle or bulls but that he should lay hand on the only thing that gives him happiness; the miracle he had waited all his life and the inheritor of all that he has been laboring for – even ISAAC. Gen. 22: 2. What a humbling experience, a temptation of the highest order, but glory is to God that Abraham believed God to the later and was regarded by God as righteous. We should realize that while Abraham was counted as a righteous person before God, the principles of the law and human ethics condemned Abraham for his action – for the law did not conditionally forbid murder. So whether God had spoken or that the devil had ministered, the law has it in its code of conduct – you must not commit murder!

Children are automatic inheritors of their biological parents, however, in Abraham's era, the righteousness of

God also worked against the natural law. What kind of a God would make life that uncomfortable for his worshipper and still the man continues to follow patiently? Can you see why Abraham was different from you and me? But we must come to the level of Abraham's conviction before God can also approve us. Sometimes it borders me how a person would leave his own homeland away from his kinsmen and relatives not knowing where he was going but yet he kept on moving at the commandment of the LORD. Gen. 12:1. It was not just for one single time that the faith of the man of God, Abraham, was put to the test but in all, Abraham believed God, that God was so excited of such obedience from mortal man that HE took Abraham as HIS best friend. Gen. 15:6, Jams 2: 23.

God did not credit righteousness to Abraham merely because he abstained from sin, but Abraham qualified to be the father of the faithful because he obeyed God in all circumstances. Abraham did not question the instruction to murder his only son, Isaac, because it came from God since he was ready and prepared to do anything to and for God.

The righteousness of God does not always work in line with the righteousness belonging to man. The thing that man may despise and consider to be sinful may turn out to be righteousness in the face of God depending on the circumstance. God is loving and abundant in mercy but will never justify the wicked but certainly will reward every man according to what he had labored with his hands. When God chooses to punish the ways of the wicked, it takes sound spiritual understanding for neighbors around to comprehend or else such may be caught in unrighteousness before God through their extreme sympathy; considering themselves more merciful than God. A lot of people have lost the position the LORD gave to them; some have even paid with their own lives when they try to stand against the LORD when HE rises to destroy the wicked. What do you think would have happened to the man or woman who saw Ananias fall and die after lying before the Holy Spirit? Maybe such runs and tells the wife Saphirah what happened – the one would definitely become a partaker in the wickedness and will receive his/her punishment. Saul, the king of Israel would show piety on the nation the LORD had judged and therefore paid with his kingdom; for the righteousness of God at the time was that the Amalekites should no more exist. Ex. 32:27-29, 1 Sam. 15: 18 –23.

If any one works contrary to the righteousness belonging to God in his circumstance, such individual will certainly lose his salvation no matter his background. That is the reason why that sound obedience is required of us when we are following God because we cannot be acknowledged by God, as was Abraham, if we cannot stop when God wants us to stop and move only at HIS command.

Moses was a man that was commended by God Himself so highly, with a distinction of character that every other messenger, prophet or king, will receive of the LORD through dreams and vision but only Moses would ever have had the opportunity of coming closer to God in friendly encounter. God made this statement over Moses on the condition of the faithfulness in Moses, which HE witnessed in time past and the statement remained effective as long as Moses was careful to abide in the program of God. Num. 12:6-8.

Moses was never a care-free person but one that would obey God's instruction to the later, but in one occasion he had an oversight: for the LORD would have the man Moses to meet HIM at the Horeb mountain with his rod in his hand, and what that is required of Moses by God, was to hit the rock with his rod and water will come out for the people to drink. This was neatly done and the result was perfect and every emotion and thirsts were filled. Ex. 17:6.

On another occasion a similar but different instruction came from the LORD to Moses: this time the man of God would take his rod along side with his brother Aaron with the assembly gathered to witness the demonstration of the power of God. Moses was then required to just tell the rock to bring out water in the name of the LORD, who is not a god of the rod, but Moses did otherwise like in the first instance and was not careful to follow the later instruction. Num. 20:8. Instead of Moses following the latter instructions carefully and precisely, the offenses of the children of Israel blocked his good sense of judgment and pride crept into his soul immediately: no more was the LORD the one giving HIS people water to drink instead, Moses found himself taking the position of GOD MOST HIGH and the jealousy of GOD busted in fury against the man and his brother. I believe that Moses was not condemned in the spiritual when he had stricken the rock the first time but when water did not come, that ought to have worked as a reminder to him that he was acting wrongly so as to retreat immediately but instead, he went further and stroke the rock a second time to preserve his pride before the people as a miracle worker, he already claimed. Num. 20:10, 11. The LORD at this point saw great disappointment in Moses and all his meekness were never remembered. Let us get at the point and not assume in our hearts that God treated Moses unfairly. In fact, the judgment of God over Moses should be a point of reference and encouragement to every one of us that the faithfulness of God endures forever and HE gives equal opportunity to all men. It tells us that a one time wicked man, who genuinely repents and turns away completely from his wicked ways and follows the LORD, will certainly save his soul and at the same time we are warned not to consider the calling of God as a license for lawlessness and pride. Num. 20:12. Moses did not enter into the land of promise just because he committed some kind of unrighteousness that boarders within the community of man but because he was disobedient to the jealous righteousness belonging to God!

When Christ Jesus came, as was spoken by the prophets of old, of whom Moses and other prophets bore testimony of how God will raise up for all mankind, a prophet, greater than Moses. God wanted the Israelites who so much desired to worship Moses as an idol, to worship this prophet according to the desires that has been in them from ages but regrettably, the desirous man choose otherwise since it was a commandment from the LORD. Have you not reflected on the fact that if God had truly ordained pagan holidays like Christmas and Easter – man will never have cherished it like it is done today! Acts 3:22, 23. Our Lord Jesus Christ though was God, yet for the salvation of me and my brethren took the form of mortal man and had his dwelling among flesh. The mortality of Jesus Christ during his three years and half active service and his successful accomplishment of the Ministry, graduated our Lord to satisfy the Divine necessity, which required a perfect sacrifice of none other than mortal Jesus in order to be able to hook back to the immortal FATHER, for the completion of the salvation program of man.

For thirty-three years and half, our Savior Jesus Christ was busy teaching and unveiling mysteries of the righteousness belonging to GOD and man, which he summarized by his unique way of life. The miracles, signs and wonders which our Lord performed were aimed at making the life of the fallen man meaningful and to assure the true believer that though the kingdom of this earth is presently in the hands of Satan, the devil, yet, case is different with those who have faith in God and believe in Christ Jesus. No matter how much people may discourage you or situations may tend to move your faith, just hold on like Jairus and definitely you will smile home with your miracle. Luke 8:50. There is every need for you and me to have faith in God through Christ Jesus because we have the opportunity to live right and obtain salvation only as long as life remains in us and while we abide in the LORD. When we transit from this life to beyond, the opportunity is lost and lost forever therefore, we should utilize the authorities of our faith to bring down every obstruction in our way, destroy all the mountains before us and fill every valley the enemy had dug that we may have a smoother journey through our salvation mission. Matt. 17:17-20. Anyone that would follow the social and moral teachings of Christ Jesus word-for-word would certainly prosper materially but we, the saints of the Most High, are called not only to succeed in the things of this life but most importantly that we may first discover and apprehend the life of the coming utopian reign of GOD, eternally. John 10:10.

As Jesus was anxiously establishing and demonstrating the righteousness belonging to man he was spiritually alert as to be able to yielding himself to the righteousness of God, because in it will he be exalted.

The things that our Lord Jesus Christ did to earn himself the righteousness of God include among others:

1.   TOTAL DEPENDENCY ON THE FATHER

Jesus Christ while on his earthly Ministry did not exercise himself independently; though He could be independent if He wanted, rather, our LORD was loyal to the FATHER in all things. Whatever teaching and presentation Jesus Christ delivered were according to the will of the FATHER. For the Jews would like to know who the Lord Jesus was and He affirmed that He was and is the Messiah, the Christ of God, but they will never believe Him because they knew who Mary His mother was and every history of the LORD'S background were never hidden. Our LORD made the Jews realize that He had some personal opinion that He could share concerning the way of life of His arrogant brethren but He would not cease the opportunity but would rather prefer to say only what has been authorized

Him by the FATHER. Our LORD did all these to prove a point to the watching Jews and the rest of the world that the FATHER is very reliable and monitors every activity of man. The doubt of the Jews would not stop the miracle of GOD and even if they would finally kill the Messiah as they were planning at that point, the LORD warned them that it will be then will they confirm that what He was saying was true. John 8:25-28.

2.   BAPTISM IN WATER

Our Lord Jesus Christ was born through the power of the Holy Spirit of God and with every feelings of the natural man. All aspects of man was in the Lord Jesus Christ: he could feel pains when hurt, become tired after a busy day and even get hungry for food and so the things concerning man was never a strange phenomenon with our MASTER. Heb. 4:15. For thirty years, our Lord was busy fighting with the devil against his lust and passions; and He overcame the evil one by not yielding to sin. It was because Jesus Christ did not corrupt himself with sin that made our LORD to qualify to be a propitiation for our sins. For this reason the scriptures are but guiding tools to help each and every one of us live and overcome the driving forces of sin but if by some omission we fall into sin we are also encouraged not to give-up to our struggle to reach perfection because the same Jesus Christ is out there in the spirit soliciting in our favor. For the sacrifice of the blood of Jesus Christ is most powerful, we cannot comprehend, and it is able to wash us clean again. At the same time our Lord Jesus Christ is now holding the FATHER from consuming our world not with-standing that we have gone worse than those in the days of Noah and invented wickedness more than Sodom and Go-morrah. 1 John 2:1, 2. Our Lord had to be baptized in the river Jordan not because he needed repentance like other Jews or to wash away his personal transgressions rather, our Lord needed baptism because He was to be made sin for our

51

sake. Had it been sin was found in our Lord Jesus Christ, His blood could not have had the power to carry the sin of other people because of the guilt of transgression. To bring the idea home a little so we can understand the issue more adequately: we are all aware that once a person is convicted and given prison sentence his/her civil rights are suspended. The individual cannot sue or advocate for other people while serving jail term but only an innocent citizen whose rights has been infringed upon can sue or be sued. So, no other man could have been able to pay the price of sin because even if the person chooses to die like our Lord Jesus Christ, except while the fellow had lived righteously in this life, his death is useless. 2 Cor. 5: 21. Most importantly, our LORD was baptized because he MUST satisfy the righteousness of GOD and at the same time establish a standard for mankind, as it relates to the issue of salvation. That was the very reason why Jesus took the pain and expense to journey from Galilee unto Jordan, to John the Baptist, and asked for His baptism. Mighty Jesus by this confirmed that our God has no respect for any man and so while He could do without the baptism of John yet, the FATHER already had established a single salvation program, which every man born of woman must undergo as to come into HIS Kingdom. If our Lord Jesus Christ, not withstanding that He knew no sin yet needed baptism and humbled himself to John who was inferior to Him therefore, there can be no exemption of any man, if salvation must be reached. Matt. 3:13-15.

3.   ABSOLUTE YEILDING TO THE LEADING OF THE SPIRIT

Jesus Christ is the fulfillment of all prophecies, from old, today and until the consummation of civilization; however, the leading of the Spirit of God is one of the things that distinguish the true prophets from the false prophets. For a truth, Jesus Christ while in his earthly ministry, depended wholly on the FATHER; obeyed unto baptism in water; and very importantly yielded to the leading of the Spirit.

When the Spirit leads a man there is always confusion in the *natural* of his composure. The Holy Spirit has the strongest power more than the hardest drug ever used by man and that is the reason why a person that is filled by the power must not have any dealing with sin or else it could kill more than the most perfected killing machine!

Imagine the leading of the Spirit in the life of the Israelites of old, they would move as the Pillar of Fire or Cloud sets out and would remain in a particular place as long as the Pillar of Fire or Cloud remained. A journey that could have taken some few days on a straight road, by the leading of the Spirit of God, lasted for many years. Num. 9:17. How about God's dealings with His prophets, is they're anything wrong for a person to be called a prophet of God? But do we really understand what it takes to be a true prophet? You automatically became specimen for experimentation of every step the LORD GOD would take towards blessing or cursing those you are taking prophetic message to. When God speaks to a prophet, a duty is laid on the one to bring the information of the Most High to the vivid imaginations of the people or person for which the LORD had spoken concerning; even if it will mean that the prophet himself would give his/herself to some king of physical humiliation. All these are done that man may not have any excuse whatsoever for not heeding to the instructions of God because the prophets and their humiliations will stand always to judge the disobedience of their generation and in so doing the prophet would have saved his/her own life. For when a prophet receives a message from God and keep such message to his/herself and did not do much to communicate the counsel of God; situation would go out of hand and certainly the judgment of God will take its course but God will require the ailing situation from the hands of the prophet. The reason is that prophecy do not come for the fun of it but a signal of impending danger or sign of approaching blessing, which informs man to be ready to receive the coming blessing or to do something to stop approaching danger. Ezek 4:9-15, 3:17-21. But what has the prophet done to deserve all these troubles? What can make any man accept to comply with these instructions, if not the empowerment and the ennoblement of the Holy Spirit of God?

Have you ever considered what the great men of God in old times went through to satisfy the righteousness of God in their circumstances; compare and contrast with the life of Christ Jesus, relate also to the apostles and then to your own lifestyle, today? Have you ever imagined; if these people would enter to a particular Kingdom of God because of their faithfulness – then where will you be? Let us just look at another prophet of God, the man Hosea, who lived in the Old Testament when the law forbade men from taking wives that were not virgins. But coming to this prophet who must have lived a humble and preserved life; the same LORD commanded him to take a whore for wife just because the people of Israel were living casually and prostituting themselves with idols. Hos. 1:2. What will be your reaction to the commandment of God if you were the prophet Hosea? Obey the word of God or just rebuke the Spirit and decree it shall not be your portion? Mortal man does not know the way he must follow in order to reach eternal life; therefore there is the need for the leading of the Spirit. When the Spirit truly comes to lead, he almost always walks contrary to the wishes and aspiration of man, bringing strange things across the way, but yet, carefully working towards the goal, in a way man cannot decipher. This is the reason why there are no accidents in the way of any man or woman of God but everything coming your way have been divinely programmed to bringing you into the purpose of God for you. However the devil would like to use your errors in the past to hunt you against your future glory – never ever give-in. Rom 8:28.

The Holy Spirit of God which came measurelessly upon Christ Jesus instead of taking Jesus Christ into posterity and abundance went to the opposite direction and lo, demand was laid on the LORD by the same Spirit to fast for a period of forty days and forty nights; cut off from the love and care of Mary and other of His step brothers and sisters and away in the wildlife. After the fasting was over, the same Spirit persuaded the Lord Jesus Christ to wait until He has been tempted and proven. Matt. 4:1. Does that surprise anybody? Do we not know that the Holy Spirit, as a teacher, teaches and also evaluates his students as to knowing the level of their comprehension? A good teacher will always give his students some examinations after having delivered the required curriculum. Sometimes teachers do put across smart questions, not that they are doing such to fail their students but to measure the comprehension and aptitude of such students and the beginning of success of every student is the acceptance of this truth. If a student would think otherwise and consider the teacher as, harvesting where he did not sow, that student is failed already. 1Cor. 2:13. So, we should always learn to be patient when temptations come our way and never to blame God. Almost always, the filling of the Holy Spirit of God comes through trials and temptations because the Spirit is directly opposite to materialism and the material work against the Spirit – the two will always clash when they are made to come in contact with each other within the soul of any man. Therefore to save yourself from the troubles of suffering like the grasses, where two big elephants fight, do all to determine who you will pay your allegiance to, the Spirit or the flesh. Gal. 5:17.

When the time came that Jesus Christ was to be tried and tested per his vocation, it was the Holy Spirit that took him into the desert, requiring that he fast for a period of forty days so that he could be tempted by the devil. It was the same Holy Spirit after observing a successful ministering of our Lord Jesus Christ saw that time was mature for him to be glorified and therefore, the same incited the Jews to rise against our LORD. The Holy Spirit was also responsible of moving the betrayer, Judas Iscariot to act timely, and when all have been perfected, the same authority also empowered our LORD to announce to us that the work for our salvation has successfully been concluded. John 13:27, 19:30.

4.   ACCEPTING TO DIE IN THE PLACE OF SINNERS

Our Lord Jesus Christ brought hope to hopeless man and in taking to himself the sinful position of Adam man had redemption. Like Isaac who yielded himself to his weak and old father, Abraham, because the LORD had so commanded, even so, our Lord Jesus Christ was willing and out of his personal volition submitted himself unto the will of the FATHER. It was the Lord Jesus Christ who laid down his life, and not because the Jews were stronger and more powerful to subdue Him. We should also follow this good example and boldly choose by ourselves the Kingdom of God and not to let our faith lean on another person's or allow our hearts to be cheated with some idols and/or expectations, on which we will condition our salvation. John 10:17, 18. It is sometimes exciting to challenge God by saying something like this, *"O LORD, if you will do this thing for me, I will certainly worship and serve you for the rest of my life."* It could work out sometimes that God may respond to a prayers like this but that understanding could be very dangerous where it becomes the way the person chooses to prove the faithfulness of God. It could take a person away from believing in God into compelling God to believe in him, which is a sin against the righteousness belonging to God. After the resurrection of our Lord and

Savior, Jesus Christ; which made him return to his former position in the family of God, yet has our Lord continued to subject himself to the FATHER until today and ever will remain. Through all eternity the LORD will always humble Himself to the FATHER who has made the glorification of our Lord Jesus Christ, a possibility. The LORD will never rise against the FATHER like Lucifer because while our LORD was given a name higher than every other name; made to be the LORD of lords, these subordinates, do not include the very FATHER who HIMSELF performed the miracle. 1 Cor. 15:27, 28.

CHAPTER 5

RIGHTEOUSNESS BELONGING TO GOD AS IT RELATES WITH THE CHURCH

After our Lord Jesus Christ fulfilled the law and the prophets in his own soul, he went further and established his body as a symbol of life eternity, otherwise known as the *Church*; fulfilling the scripture and words of the prophets that long ago were ringing and announcing the time to come when God would unite the hearts of HIS people by giving them more than just conscience, a time man would experience the indwelling of the Holy Spirit of God like never before. A coming era where humanity again would have the compassion and love of God which would make them treat life with the dignity it deserves that in turn would affect other creatures or the neighbors of man, into such a joy because the same salvation also has reached unto them from man. Ezek. 11:19. Our Lord turned the physical temple worship in Jerusalem into a spiritual Body comprising of individuals who have dedicated their lives unto God. A strong prophetic statement was made by our LORD concerning the destruction of the Temple of God built by Solomon in Jerusalem. Within a period of three days our Lord Jesus Christ went into the spiritual and completed the building of the CHURCH, which is the new Temple of God; not built with human hands. John 2:19, 20. So, brothers we should be glad and not loss the vision of the new Temple of God and let not any among us look down on his own self because your body and my own body is that new Temple of the Holy Spirit of God which makes it an offense before God for us to consider the life we live from now on as our own. 1 Cor. 6:19.

Our Lord did not perform this functional righteousness because it was needful for him personally rather, our Lord was establishing a standard and pre-requisition for entering into everlasting life. So when we read and study about the life and ministry of our Lord Jesus Christ, we should do so with the view of learning and copying the same way of life – doing and discharging our duties correspondingly to the manners in our LORD. 1 Pet. 2:21. Whenever we are faced with some challenges in life or are tempted by the devil in any way we should stop and ask ourselves, if it were the LORD what will He do in this circumstance? When we are sincere to listen to the inner voice in us we already has began living like the Lord Jesus Christ.

While Jesus Christ was physically present on planet earth, our Lord made lots of expressions as he heard from the FATHER. Some of these expressions were pointing to the righteousness of God which mortal man must obtain in order to enter into everlasting life.

Our LORD, through the Comforter revealed to His Church six fundamental things that would earn man the righteousness belonging to God. These include: Total Dependency on Jesus Christ; That God is able to do what He says He will do; Baptism into the Father; Baptism into the Son; Baptism by the Holy Spirit and Baptism into Fire.

1.   TOTAL DEPENDENCY ON JESUS CHRIST

Our Lord Jesus Christ had many things he could have said but never exercised himself so to; instead, he depended solely and wholly on the FATHER. Since Jesus Christ was God revealed in the flesh and whereas he is the author and finisher of our faith therefore, we, the church are duty bound to depend totally on Jesus Christ. It is sinful for mortal man to suggest to the faith or to modify the doctrine; we must abide in the doctrine and faith of our Lord Jesus Christ exactly as they were handed over to us through the apostles and prophets. We must be committed to preserving the unity in the Body of Christ by allowing His peace to shine on us through our obedience to His Word. Our knowledge and understanding that there is only one nation in Christ Jesus and that we have earned our Heavenly nationality through the doctrine of truth; helps us a lot so that we might be able to have the mustard seed faith which will make us to be very eager to receive the baptisms that would in turn covenant us with the FATHER ALMIGHTY in Christ Jesus. Eph. 4:3-6.

Our Lord Jesus Christ is the only eyewitness to the personality of the FATHER ALMIGHTY. John 1:18. Jesus Christ bore witness of the FATHER whom He had seen and been acquainted with and have declared unto us the little we should know for now. Like it is with the Father and Son, so also, it is with Christ Jesus and His apostles, therefore must we (the church) bear witness of Christ Jesus through following meticulously the doctrines of the apostles which was revealed through prophesy. We should not assume what the FATHER could be, lest we fall into condemnation but rather we should base our understanding on the evidence at hand – JESUS CHRIST'S testimony. Ephs. 3:4, 5.

For us to have the righteousness belonging to God, we must depend wholly on the teachings of Christ Jesus, as we read that the apostles practiced. When we have been able to completely divorce ourselves from adding or subtracting to/from the unity of faith, then can we be considered righteous before God!

2. BELIEVING THAT GOD IS ABLE TO DO WHAT HE SAYS HE WILL DO

It is very simple for any man or woman to try and live right; abstaining from adultery and other related sins but it takes faith for mortal man to believe that God is able to do what HE says HE will do. It is not very convenient to believe that just the mark of blood upon the lintel will save the entire household and not having blood upon the lintel means death and destruction. Can you imagine Moses bringing out water from the rock through hitting at one time, and coming to another time; just him speaking to the rock becomes what was needed to bring out so much water and because he hit the rock, instead, sin that cannot be pardoned, was imputed on him. In all these and more, it takes faith to move mountains because it is when a person has the faith and believe that God does exist, not doubting in his mind, that such could be encourage to getting into the various adventures needed by the doctrine and with the experimentations and results the one will substantiate the realities of God. Heb. 11:6.

Many confessing believers do not understand that Christ Jesus brought a new and living way to God. Some are yet to know that there is the *milk-gospel* and *solid-gos-*

pel. Too many, out of share negligence being infants, yet they ignore the *milk-gospel* and *stumble* over *solid gospel.* When a child is newly born and feeble he feeds only on liquid foods and cannot eat bone or take in solid food; the same is applicable to a person who has just been adopted into the family of the Heavenly, the person need to be educated on the fundamentals principles in his new life and gradually introduced into the deep mysteries of the Kingdom of God else, he will stumble thereby. But we all must do all within our reach to have the right spiritual food as to enable us to grow in grace and knowledge of God unto a full man, able to differentiate between the good and the evil. Do you know that it is not an easy task to know the good from the evil: many today are sincerely wrong, doing wickedly but not knowing they are in error – maturity in man comes when he can truly and fairly discern the right from the wrong. Heb. 5:11-14.

The milk-gospel is the bedrock of believer's salvation, which each and everyone that embraces the truth must first experience. The milk gospels include: the infantry teachings concerning Christ Jesus, how He walked closely with the FATHER and was lifted up against every authority and power; the necessity of repentance from the works that lead to death; encouragement to have faith that God has the ability to deliver; acceptance to be initiated into the Body of Christ through the baptisms; yielding to the doctrine of Holy Spirit impartation by the laying on of hands and believing that the dead will rise again to face God's judgment. This is the basic of every believer's salvation and is the milk gospel that the young in the faith must feed on as to grow adequately. Heb. 6:1, 2.

It is wonderful for any man to obtain repentance to such degree that would draw him away from all manners of unrighteousness. When challenges come in the way of the believer, nothing else could be done than to pray and for the prayer to be effective, there must be faith in God.

The bible outlines four baptisms namely the *baptism of the Father, the baptism of the Son, the baptism of the Holy Spirit* and then *baptism of fire*. John the Baptist bore witness that this is true. To be able to believe on these divine purposes and to follow carefully the way they were handled by the apostles earns one the righteousness belonging to God. Matt. 28:19, Matt. 3:11.

3.   BAPTISM INTO THE NAME OF THE FATHER

From the day the generation of man was established in Adam and Eve, the man was right with God equipped with every instrument he needed to be the son of God - even the Holy Spirit. Gen. 2:7. Looking closely to this scripture we would observe two prominent things namely, the touching of the dust by God and then the impartation of the Holy Spirit.

After man fell off the grace of God and returned back to earth, there was the need to gather the dust back by the second touch of God. In fact, the sin of disobedience put the man out of spiritual balance making it of a necessity that God personally will be involved from the inception of the recovering process. The heart of man is the center point of this baptism into the FATHER: it was the heart of man that Satan the devil conquered and overcame with sin, therefore, the inception of man's recovery can start from none other than this. The human heart is so complicated and dangerous that the wisest of the wise has been eluded, for no man can tell what could be in the heart of any man. This is why the civilization of man would continue to be pre-occupied with the challenges of how to manage violence and crime – all this begins in the heart of man. Jer. 17:9. The prophecies of old are fulfilled today as the perfect will and desire of God

64

is done on behalf of us the elect whom He gives conviction as to receive the miracle of Repentance. The heart of man in the spirit could be seen polluted with dirt ranging from adultery, evil thoughts, lust, jealousy, pride, arrogance and so on, with all these the man can in no wise be made at peace with God. The prophet Ezekiel however saw the miracle we have received today through Christ Jesus, who has by His life, death and resurrection given us the opportunity to have a new heart which could be washed clean away from dirt, anytime, now. Ezek. 36:25. The clean water according to this prophecy is the gospel of our Lord Jesus Christ which is preached in season and out of season; the idols are those covenants that hold men bound in the *Adamic* sin and the new heart is the gift of REPENTANCE which is receivable only from God and to whom He wills.

A sinner hearing the gospel of Jesus Christ can never believe except a second touch of God comes from Heaven and convicts the sinner and spiritually the individual is born into the FATHER. For it was the same gospel preached by our Lord Jesus Christ which made people like Peter, Matthew and so on to become faithful disciples and at the same time provoked other Jews to crucify the LORD. The difference is simple, God touched the first but the later never had their eyes opened. 1 John 5:1.

Not everyone that hears the gospel of Truth believes and those that believe do so not because they have greater wisdom or brighter understanding than others but because it pleases God to grant favor to such individuals. The opportunity to believe in the foolishness of what that is preached comes from the FATHER unto whom ever HE wills, even our Lord Jesus Christ, does not have the power to convict any man and bring such to repentance. John 6:43-45, 1 Cor. 1:21.

The truth of the gospel does not wear tangible glory and there is no physical attractiveness that may encourage the sinner to believe, except the Lord God turns the heart-key of any man and baptizes such with the gift of REPENTANCE, such cannot REPENT. Is. 53:2, John 6:65.

After God had honored a sinner with the gift of repentance, such must believe the good news with a renewed hope that a wretched and miserable sinner can be turned around into a saint. Salvation is a gift that begins with the baptism into the FATHER. In the baptism of the Father the whole work is done by the ETERNAL FATHER through the preaching of the gospel of Jesus Christ; which signifies the exclusive building of man in the day of creation, being that man did not offer any assistance to God in making creation a possibility therefore, man can do nothing in other to receive repentance. On the other hand, the dust that was taken by God was carefully selected out of the earth. Not all the dust upon the earth was taken by God to form man; this goes on to reveal the mystery of predestination in God's salvation plan. The whole world is filled with dustmen, among whom the God Almighty by His choice and Divinity is choosing men among the dustmen, of whom He will use to build into the man (Christ Jesus). To make this great call of the LORD possible each and every one of us has his/her own testimony of how the miracle of salvation came about to the saving of our souls. Sometimes the incident may not be a happy and pleasurable one but God will always design a man's salvation plan to be unique and different from another; just as the finger prints of two individuals can never be the same." Rom. 8:28, 29.

Baptism into the name of the Father is that spiritual exercise significant of dipping sinful man into the Creator, otherwise called - REPENTANCE!

66

4.   BAPTISIM INTO THE NAME OF THE SON

How can mortal man be baptized into the name of the Son?

To help in this our study, let us again look at what baptism is all about, perhaps from another different perspective and then what the name of the Son is.

Baptism means, to dip or to be buried into!

Today's controversies of whom and what the name of the FATHER and HIS SON is, were seen from prophetical times of old. But who can tell the name of the FATHER, except the SON and what is the name of the SON – He is Jesus, the Christ of God. Prov. 30:4, Matt. 16:13-16. Many do not recognize Jesus, as the Christ of God, even today: by what they preach, teach and the doctrine they confess, and worst is that they accept the mockery name of the antichrist, CHRISTIANITY.

After God made and glorified man with the favors of an already made garden and the pleasantries of life, there was the need to test human obedience in which process the man failed. It was because of the failure of man that the Holy Spirit which he received on the day he was made was withdrawn. Gen 6:3. Since the Holy Spirit left man because he could not abide in the works of obedience, whenever the same man will be restored, certainly the man must be tested and proven to be obedient. On the other hand, there was some condemnation that required cleansing, which only the SON could be found worthy to risk his own life for. Matt. 20:28. Erasing the condemnation against human race through his blood, therefore, everyone that believes in the gospel of truth **MUST – turn away from following the devil and receive the cleansing of sin through baptism in water in the name of Jesus Christ so that the dirt in the**

soul of the man may be wiped away as to make way for the infilling of the Holy Spirit of God. Acts 2:38.

With old Israel, Sabbath keeping was the test commandment, which the Israelites did not abide in; coming to the new covenant of grace, another simplified test commandment was given. Mark 16:16. To show that this is a test commandment that requires some work from man, our Lord, Jesus Christ showed us example, traveling all the way from Galilee to Jordan for no other purpose but to be baptized by John. Matt. 3:13. Though He was greater and more honorable than John yet, our Lord Jesus Christ did not wait or send some people to bring John to him in Galilee or ask that John would have to pay for the cost of his transportation being the Master rather, just as other Jews were coming on their own accord to be baptized so also did our LORD take the full duty on Himself.

It seems that God would always like to test man; maybe because God would have man come into an estate of glory and honor therefore, must the man undergo several tests and examinations and cross-examinations. Gen 2:16, 17. Particularly speaking, it was man's disobedience in this area that turned man into enemy of God. The keeping of the later test commandment in the new covenant by our Lord Jesus Christ brought two primary things, namely: *prove of man's obedience to God* and then *remedy for offenses.*

Believing the wholesome truth to the level of being baptized in water in the name of Jesus Christ sound weak and simple but remains the hardest and most difficult thing any mortal man can do, rightly.

The obedience of Adam and Eve were tested exclusively in the Garden of Eden. Even where there could be fruits that have physical resemblance with the tree of good and evil, the commandment was effective only in the garden, Eden. Adam and Eve, after the incident in Eden may decide not to eat fruits that look like the forbidden fruit, yet that can never earn them righteousness because the righteousness of God work in accordance to the time and place it has been designed for, by God. In the same way, the doctrine of baptism only works when the one true Body of Christ does it, in its proper way, and at the right time. Eph. 4:4-6.

When a person is soaked into Christ Jesus, the individual becomes a partaker in the life, death and resurrection of Christ Jesus. Gal. 3:27. In the side of Christ's death and resurrection, we were buried with Him through baptism that we also might join with Him in resurrecting, with a resultant effect that our lifestyle would change for the better. Rom. 6:3, 4.

5.   BAPTISM INTO THE NAME OF THE HOLY SPIRIT.

What is the name of the Holy Spirit?

The Holy Spirit is the power in God, which can be extended to mortal man in order to bring such into the family of God. It is this Holy Spirit of God that bears witness in the spiritual that we are children of God, after we have been careful to obey all that our LORD commanded us. It also lead and direct the path of the church through the rough and rouged way of salvation into the Kingdom of God, giving us the boldness to call the FATHER of our Lord Jesus Christ our own FATHER. Rom. 8:15, 16.

To dip one into the power belonging to God is different from receiving the Holy Spirit.

Let us consider the calling of Moses for example, first of all God had to appoint Moses directly from Heaven as a leader of the nation of God. Ex.3: 7, 10. After that, there was the need again for the same Moses to be commissioned by God to the noble task of bringing the children of God out of bondage, and to command the full authorities of God there was also the need for the man to be filled with the power of God. Ex. 4:1-9.

In the same way our Lord Jesus Christ had to directly appoint His original disciples whom He also commissioned on the day of Pentecost. John 20:21-23, Act 2:1-4. And to be sure there is equality between the Jews and the Gentiles; the same LORD that gave His power directly to the Jews also poured His power to open the way for the Gentiles, so in the house of Cornelius the miracle that brought us, the Gentiles, happened. Acts 10:44-47. With Christ Jesus both the Jews and the Gentiles are going to be justified by one divine standard – faith. Rom. 3:27-30. God did not make the Gentile world to experience the Holy Spirit via the Jews; rather, the same Holy Spirit that came upon the Jews on the day of Pentecost also was made available to the Gentiles in the house of Cornelius.

I will like to briefly comment on two very important aspects of Christ Jesus' Ministry and the establishment of the Church. A close observation would reveal the mystery of Christ Jesus, standing as the embodiment of both the old and new covenant. Many people today do not realize that Christ Jesus did not work exclusively for the new covenant, but rather, our LORD first of all fulfilled the old covenant before transiting into the new.

To begin the miraculous old covenant that was to last for some period of three and half years, our LORD called His twelve apostles to become the instrument He will use to save the children of the covenant from the bondage of Satan just as God called Moses. Luke 6:13, Matt. 10: 6. This was the beginning of the miraculous Old Testament in Christ

Jesus. After which also, the LORD commissioned these twelve into the service of the Ministry when they were yet to receive the Holy Spirit power, which now perfected the old covenant in Christ Jesus that previously was imperfect in Moses. Matt. 10:8. This marked the ending of the old covenant in Christ Jesus.

Going further our LORD decided to establish a brand NEW COVENANT in His blood and after He had finished the work on Calvary, He called the same disciples and made them receive the authority to enter into the Kingdom of God and also be instrumental to bringing other people into the glorious life to come. John 20: 22, 23. This also marks the beginning of the NEW COVENANT. This apostles and disciples He also commissioned to the service of the NEW COVENANT on the day of Pentecost. Act. 2: 1-4. While Jesus Christ was still alive, the operational covenant that He also administered was but the covenant of the old and not until his death and resurrection did our LORD institute the new covenant, which made Him the fulfillment of both the old and new covenants.

Our LORD was never joking or making proverbial statement when He spoke of building the Temple in just three days but the truth remain that the Messiah went into the spiritual and perfected the work of God by His obedience. Remember that originally God told Moses that the journey from Egypt into the land of promise will last only three days but because of the disobedience of the children of Israel couple with their unbelief, this journey took many years. When Jesus Christ came and obeyed every aspect of the commandment of God, the faithful FATHER prove to the world and the spirits that HE never lied and for just three days, Jesus Christ took the church from the kingdom of Satan and brought them into the paradise of God. Ex. 3: 18, John 2:19.

Men cannot believe if there is not the demonstration of God's power; after all, it is not possible that God, the Creator of the whole Universe to be present in a place or circumstance without making the difference. Therefore, on the day of Pentecost the power of God filled the apostles and disciples and great signs and wonders followed. After the apostles received the confirmation of their ordination into their calling according to the word of our Master Jesus Christ, as it is written in the book of John 20 verse 21-23, the apostles did not start going out but waited for the baptism of the Holy Spirit – that is the empowerment or commissioning. Paul, the apostle of the Lord Jesus Christ, did not just preach the gospel of our LORD for the fun of it rather; with every enthusiasm he was bold knowing he had the power. 1 Cor. 2:4.

After Moses received the commissioning and power from God, those that worked with Moses needed not to go and obtain their own authority directly from God rather; they were to receive their commissioning through the laying on of hands of Moses. God did this so that HE can easily control HIS people with one language commandment and at the same time have a particular person HE would hold accountable to the activities of the people. Christ Jesus is the one held responsible to the activities of the church today and the apostles in conjunction with the prophets are those that we look on to physically in the church today, who shall also render account unto Christ Jesus. John 17: 12, Heb. 13: 17.

To receive the Holy Spirit, the old time doctrine of impartation, from the man already filled to another prepared to receive, remain unchanged. Num. 27:18-20. There can never be another way to approach things that relate to Jehovah God except by obeying the Word; for Joshua was able to exploit for the LORD even after Moses the servant of

God was dead; not just because he was smart but because he already received the authority and power. Deut. 34:9.

The Kingdom of God is one and therefore those that shall enter into it must be united from this life into the world to come; there are lots of breaches that must be bridged, gaps that must be filled and differences that need to be duly reconciled. There must be some significant and noticeable differences in a man when his former life is compared with the life he lives after he has come into the faith of Christ Jesus. If the man continues to live as before and perhaps the only experience of Christ in his life which he can testify is only a sudden financial breakthrough in his business, without the circumcision of the heart, such has acquired some chronic spiritual disease that maybe very hard to cure. Eph. 2:11, 13 &14. Prosperity in the things of this life is not all that is needed as to notice the presence and manifestation of the Holy Spirit of God; it is just an auxiliary or catalyst in the life of a soul that has been regenerated. Luke 12: 15, Matt. 6: 33. There are many fruits, which a living soul must bears and without the presence of these attributes the individual who boast in the things of the flesh, will land himself in the lake of fire, afterwards. Gal. 5: 22.

The church first got baptized or dipped into the Holy Spirit on the day of Pentecost and in the house of Cornelius and having received the power, and through revelation knowledge made available by the Spirit: a way and doctrine was established in the church by which those believing will receive and be baptized into the Holy Spirit.

As a doctrine of the true church the Holy Spirit of God is passed on from one person to another through the laying on of hands of those that has been divinely called to the service of the Ministry. Acts 8:18.

After the believer has received the gift of the Holy Spirit at the laying on of the apostles' hand, it remains that such should fast and pray, waiting upon the Lord who will baptize such fellow with the Holy Spirit at Christ Jesus' own time. The first baptism in the Holy Spirit came upon Jesus' disciples who were patiently waiting for the promise and the LORD released His Spirit at His own good time and not according to the control or commandment of man. Luke 24:49, 1 Cor 14:1.

The plan and purpose of God requiring man to be dipped into the Father, Son and Holy Spirit is to assure that mortal man who is a common soul, composed of the gross matter is regenerated into a spirit being. In the discussion Jesus Christ had with Nicodemus, our LORD summarily revealed the mystery in the various baptisms. The first statement of our Master centered on the baptism into the name of the Father. John 3: 3. Regarding the baptism of the Son and the Holy Spirit, our Lord was very careful to divide the two into the dipping in water and then in the Spirit. John 3:5-7.

6.   BAPTISM INTO FIRE!

Man has a fire consumable origin that was quickened by the Holy Spirit, loaned to man by God in the day the man was made. The spirit which God gave to man could have been developed to the level of man's translation from the gross matter into spirit-being had it been the man did not fall. Coming to the case of Christ Jesus, our Lord completely obeyed the ETERNAL FATHER making the difference in between. 1 Cor. 15:45.

By the time a *soul* is born of God, sins forgiven, and is baptized into the Spirit, the man would be partly carnal and partly spirit, and since the Kingdom of God is total spirit therefore such partial man cannot enter into the kingdom

74

of God except he dies naturally. To make the partial man a complete spirit requires a burning by fire which will consume the perishable, leaving only the imperishable – this is what the baptism into fire is all about! We are being built in the spirit through the designing by the Word of God and how much we yield ourselves to the gospel will determine the kind of vessel we would represent in the house of our GOD. After we have done all, God will again evaluate our individual ministries and if we would not pass the standard test of the ALMIGHTY we are lost in the spirit. So again, that sounds another note of warning that we must not relax after obtaining salvation but should need to work even harder as to be approved by God. 1 Cor. 3:10-17.

The purpose of God bringing salvation, (i.e. Christ Jesus) unto man is that the man would not just be alive but that the man may through a workable obedience have life in abundance and meaningfully exist as the bearer of God's insignia among creation. John 10:10. Poverty, sicknesses and diseases are not the portion of children of God, and that is the reason why the saints should do all to stay away from sin so that when we pray for material blessings our faithfulness to God in the spiritual will be reflected to the things in the material. 3 John 2.

When the fire of God leaves the man a complete spirit by consuming all his carnality, there are no more battles to fight in the spirit because the war of the saints in the spirit today is to fight against the lust of the flesh and the deceitfulness of the eyes.1 John 5:4. Allow your physical side of life to be consumed totally by the fire of God so that you may come into the Holy presence of God and obtain the freedom that makes it needless for you fighting your own battle all by yourself.

Those who have overcome the world have a different language they speak because they are complete in-spirit and though they are aware that they have the authority and power to change situations through prayer, yet they have greatest respect to the will of the ETERNAL FATHER. They would make their supplication and prayers normally and present their petitions according to their heart desires but will sum up resultant with the willingness to accept the perfect will of God in each and every of their circumstances. Matt. 26:38-42.

The moment a one time believer is suffering on account of a crime he really committed or going through some kind of humiliation because of his unfaithfulness; that has nothing at all to do with the cross of our Lord Jesus Christ but the person has fallen off from the spiritual Temple which the Lord Jesus Christ built with His own body down to the tabernacles controlled by the laws of Moses. We bear the cross when we are just, yet given the fate of the unjust; when we are innocent, but made to suffer because we have been falsely condemned; it is in such circumstances that we are approved of God. 1 Peter 2:19-21. The saint may have his faith tested with poverty; sickness, disease or persecution as was in the case of Job but that does not give any man excuse to blaspheme. Job 1:8-12. If Job endured trail and temptations in old times when the Holy Spirit does not live in the human soul shall God not require of us even more consistency and sound endurance in times of temptation since we have all it takes to overcome.

If God will boast before Satan because of you, as He did in the case of Job will you be able to remain faithful or will you bring shame to the holy name of the MOST HIGH! Do you not realize that Job went through all the trials, not because he sinned against God but because God wanted to prove to Satan that a true saint is one who obeys God, unconditionally! The elect of God who knows what and who he believes in, must act maturely and be deeply rooted in faith that nothing can shake nor root him out from his standing. If you have really come to the understanding that God truly exist and is more than what has been revealed to man, then the power of the witches would have no effect on you and your inheritance. The devil's witchcraft works in the life of any man, the moment the person begins to doubt the possibilities of God and when such happens, a spirit man would become a scientist overnight – judging situations by the evidence at hand than taking the intangible advantages of faith. Rom. 8:35-39. Believe God! The moment He has spoken concerning your condition, don't let your sense of vision cheat your judgment of faith. Worries delays miracles and regret abort them and when you have been infected in your mind by worries and regrets, the next thing that the devil will suggest is for you to willingly surrender in the battle so that he will take you as prisoner of war. The enemy will never let go those he captures and the torture in his camp is unbearable; so don't you ever wish you be a victim – have faith in God. Again I adjure you, have faith in God and you will never be disappointed.

Baptism by fire is the way of the cross and after it there is a crown. As faces differ from one person to another so also shall each and every one of us go through his/her own unique way of the cross! Our LORD does not paint the truth or present the way to the Kingdom of God in a light picture rather, while He educates us on how wonderful it is to serve God; He also makes us to understand that there are also sufferings we cannot avoid which forms a part of the transition process. Luke 9:23, Act 14:22. So it is better to know the truth about this and be in the lookout for challenges and when they come instead of worrying we should rejoice and be glad and then will our miracle and deliverance hasten more to meet us. Matt. 5: 11, 12.

I would like to clarify this one important point: suffering and dilemma are not among the doctrine of the true church. The teachings of the church lie on prosperity and abundant living in righteousness. Take for instance where a brother tells lies in order to make gains or to elude some punishment, such person is yet to be baptized fully in the Holy Spirit and know nothing about the Fire baptism. A brother could be under the bondage of poverty because of the stigma of unfaithfulness. Each time there is some test in a particular area, where he/she fails – no prayer or fasting can pull such one out from the reproach of poverty except where he accepts the fire of God to consume the old self.

A person who has received the Fire baptism cannot sin consciously because he has been born into the family of God. 1 John 5:18. The saint who has been baptized with fire can suffer persecution and even tribulation not because such person committed some iniquity but because the individual holds on to righteousness not minding blood. 1 Pet. 4:12-14.

Fire baptism is a spiritual consciousness where the saint graduates to the highest attainable plain of man, a state where there is almost absolute replacement of mortality by immortality. In such situation there is total spiritual freedom by complete mortification of the flesh with consequence of the elect being liberated from prayer worries. The man is set free from the fear of death; replaced by the joy to put off mortality. Phil. 1:21.

Since the man has become spirit by the process of baptism in fire: the spirit-man, like Christ Jesus, will never withdraw himself from following after the Holy Spirit. Prophesy cannot stop the accomplishment of the desires of our LORD as may be directed by the Holy Spirit. Prophecy reveals the past; explains the present and unveils the future but cannot easily tell the mind of God. It takes a living soul to discern the perfect will of God in the middle of pressing circumstances. Agabus, the prophet of God truly saw what will happen to Paul in Jerusalem but his revelation did not say what the mind of God in the matter; whether Paul should go or forbear. So, after the prophecy, the devil started using the brethren around Paul to dissuade him just as Satan entered into Peter to attack our Lord Jesus Christ. Mark 8:33, Acts 21:10-14. At times like this it is safest to be on the LORD'S side and to do the will of the FATHER.

The mysteries and realities about the Fire baptism were made manifest and vividly revealed at the mountain. Matt. 17:2. This event was another tangible evidence that Christ Jesus though was God in the flesh, yet he yielded himself to the burning of the Spirit fire until he was completely consumed, leaving a residual of a total spirit-man. The effect of this is also noticed in the later verse. Jesus Christ graduated from being the darling of the FATHER into a commissioned inheritor. Matt. 17:5. It was after Christ Jesus had been baptized with Fire that the FATHER saw a completed Ministry and perfectly fulfilled vision of an accomplished salvation in Christ Jesus, which qualified our Lord to be the giver of life and Savior of the world.

CHAPTER 6

DISCERNING THE TRUE SALVATION

Our Lord and Savior Jesus Christ lived an exemplary life and by his death He took away the sins of the world. By his resurrection, captivity was taken captive, and living in glory he has made every other power, powerless.

Many that are confessing Christ Jesus today have limited themselves to the physical Ministry of Christ, emphasizing on the need to turn away from sin and do good. The modern day preachers have centered upon repentance. Little do they know that the physical ministry of Christ Jesus was attached with curse from the laws of Moses? The laws of Moses waged war against the personality of Christ Jesus, falsely accusing the Messiah and invoking curse on the Savior of the world. Gal. 3:13. It was because the laws of Moses were not in agreement with the law of liberty in Christ Jesus that condemnation came against the TRUTH and as a consequence, the Jews killed the Messiah.

While Jesus Christ was physically alive on planet earth, he was charged with a greater responsibility to carefully divide the old covenant so that the laws of God would stand out from the laws of Moses. This was a very wonderful task, which only a Spirit-filled Messiah like our Lord can undertake. After dividing the elements in the old covenant, and bringing out the laws of the ETERNAL and those of Moses, Christ Jesus went on and abolished the laws of Moses and the commandment of elders without any reservations. Establishing a better channel through which we can come to the Holy presence of God without having to go through the humiliations of the lies in the Mosaic concept. Heb. 7: 18, 19. On the other hand, Jesus Christ fulfilled the laws of the ETERNAL with his own body. Every commandment of God Most High exactly as Moses originally received them from Jehovah God were meticulously observed and perfected in the person of our Lord Jesus Christ. Matt. 5:17.

The physical life of Jesus Christ was a turning point from the material into the spirit, otherwise known as REPENTANCE. Our LORD in principle taught the Jews about the laws of liberty; not that the Jews would be able to embrace and practice them, but that the Jews might be witnesses to the unfading faithfulness of Jehovah God since it was their forefathers that received the law in the covenant of the old.

Seeing the limitations in man and the inability of the disciples to truly comprehend the doctrine, Christ encouraged them to wait and receive the Holy Spirit power. This power that was to come down upon the Disciples of Christ

Jesus, pluralizing the personality of the MASTER as many time as those that would believe. Therefore it will not come until the LORD had gone back to the FATHER and perfectly arranged the miracle, which will give each believer the opportunity of having Christ living in his/her personal soul – without this, man cannot make Heaven. John 16: 7.

Even our Lord needed the Holy Spirit!

Jesus Christ was able to do all that he did within the three years and half of his active ministry on earth because he first obtained the righteousness of God the Father by obeying unto baptism in the water which gave room for him to be filled with the Holy Spirit. It was also by this baptism that the LORD was able to receive the miracle of the ETERNAL FATHER coming into His soul and abiding with Him. When Christ Jesus tried to explain this miracle to the Jews, He was accused of equating Himself with the ALMIGHTY GOD that He never did. It is therefore improper for mortal man to teach or learn the life of Christ and his ministry without first receiving the righteousness that belongs to God through faith in the baptism in water and the receiving of the Holy Spirit by the laying-on of hands of the apostles.

There are missing dimensions in the way world preachers today are presenting SALVATION. We hear in our media, messages like this, *"Receive Jesus Christ as your personal Lord and Savior and you will be saved."* In crusade grounds we have noticed sinners weeping and asking, *"...what shall we do?"* Like it was with the people who were gathered on the day of Pentecost. Only a few of us seem to notice that there is stark difference between what Peter said on the day of Pentecost and what world preachers today are doing. Acts 2:38. Contrary to what Peter said and did; great preachers of the world today call sinners to their altars and lead such people to Christ through recitation like this, *"I am a sinner, I cannot help myself; I come to you Lord Jesus, I confess my sins unto you and plead that you today cancel my name in the book of death and write my name in the book of life. This I pray in Jesus name. Amen!"* The preachers will then pray on behalf of those who have answered the alter call like this, *"Lord Jesus, I present these sinners to you may it please you to forgive their sins; cancel their name in the book of death and transfer their names to your book of life and bring them into your heavenly glory, this I pray in Jesus holy name, Amen."*

Neither Christ nor the apostles presented or preached SALVATION in the manner our modern-day preachers are doing. To the contrary, the apostles upheld the earlier instructions of Christ Jesus, as it is written in the book of Mark 16:15,16. When the glorified Christ Jesus spoke to His church through the Holy Spirit on the day of Pentecost, a more vivid explanation was given of how baptism into the Father, Son and Holy Spirit could be done. Matthew 28: 18 – 20, Act 2: 38.

World messengers are preaching only REPENTANCE, which is the baptism into the Father, omitting the other baptisms. In this regard, billions of people are today identified with the Christian religion with every of their spiritual filthiness not washed away from their souls or their sins being forgiven, a fulfillment of the word of prophecy according to Proverbs 30 verse 12.

One may want to know how a person could truly realize that he/she has been saved, washed away from sin and liberated from every covenant of Satan the devil. At this point I will like to quickly say that a man's position with God or Satan can be ascertained by his posture in the spirit. No matter how spiritual a man may be in the physical or how devoted such could be to the things that pertain to God, as far as such still have some dealings with evil forces, the person remain a child of the devil. Our LORD made the Jews to know that one of the characteristics that shows that a man is of the devil is that the person would hate Christ Jesus directly or indirectly. The language in the spiritual is prophecy and no man can truly be a child of God without hearing from God and understanding the language of Christ Jesus. Those of the devil however, will always receive false messages in the spirit from the lying tongue of Satan that in turn make them false prophets. John 8: 42 - 44.

Man was created by God to exercise himself physically in his day-to-day activities and at the same time has the opportunity of communicating with the spiritual realm each time he looses consciousness in the phenomenon of sleep or some kind of trance. One could repent and be identified with some particular denomination yet, is held bound by Satan the devil. There is no other way a person may find out about this except when the individual realizes that he/she is disobedient to the word of God in times of his unconsciousness. Every action of man is first executed in the spiritual before it is shifted to the physical. For example, a person may not at a particular time be committing adultery in the physical but he/she might be held bound by the devil with the spirit of adultery, which makes the individual to have sex in the dream. This is against the Word of God, for; our Lord Jesus Christ without mincing words taught that in the spirit there is no male or female and therefore, any spirit that projects a contrary idea is of the antichrist and whoever it may be that still experiences sex euphoria in the dream is still within the kingdom of darkness and has no covenant with Christ Jesus. Luke 20:34-36. Our LORD was talking particularly concerning the sex act between man and woman, that it will not be practiced in the Kingdom of God and not just marriage because already Jesus Christ will be married to His bride, the church of the Living God. The marriage between Christ Jesus and the church has nothing to do with sex passion but could be compared to the time

85

of innocence of Adam and wife Eve – marriage is possible without sex passion. Sex was designed by God as instrument of procreation which has expiration; it is because many has misconstrued marriage to mean sex and pleasure that we are seeing so much divorce in our time like never before.

Dreams and visions is the doorway into the spiritual not minding whether a person is a child of God or not there is always these experiences. Think about the kind of dreams that you have been having and believe it or not that explains where you belong or who you are. According to the law a man or woman becomes ceremonially unclean when there is some discharge from the body of the individual and such was required by law to be purified through some seven-day period. A person would commit adultery after having been through bodily uncleanness for sometime, in which case he covenants with the devil in the spiritual. A person who commits adultery in the dream, always having nightmares or finds himself in the corridors of the kingdom of darkness can never enter into the Kingdom of God because he is defiled spiritually by the covenant with evil forces. It was basically to destroy these powers that Christ Jesus incarnated. 1 John 3:7, 8. Those who suffer from the issue of blood like the woman in Matthew 9 verse 20 or perhaps people whose ailment have defied medical principle may trace the origin of such sickness from some encounter in the dream or vision or touching by an unknown stranger. Unfortunately today's preachers say so little about the breaking of curses and the reconciliation of man with God and even when they try, they end up leading people astray. A child of God cannot have dealings with the kingdom of darkness and at the same time be at peace with God. The kingdom of darkness remain in the waters according to the revelation of the Word of God, it is therefore improper for a child of God to find his/herself in the dream, swimming, attending meetings and doing one thing or another – this shows that the soul of that individual is the property of the devil. Some cannot say

86

what really happens to them in their spiritual world because they would fly, fight, eat, party and do a lot of things, which they neither can tell the beginning nor the ending. This standard has respect of no person and if our Bishops, General Overseers and the Great men of God of our time will be sincere to themselves they would confess of their bondages with evil forces which they have nickname spiritual attack. That is not spiritual attack but a sign that you belong to the devil and you must do something now before it becomes too late. You need to wash away your sins in the lambs blood that your sins maybe forgiven you - the hard truth is that you must be baptized in the name of Jesus Christ to be able to break the covenant which you have with evil forces and then establish the new covenant of Christ in your life.

No amount of prayers, fasting or invocation can truly liberate a man from the bondages of the devil, the only permanent cure is to obey the Word of God and yield to the doctrine.

The man of wickedness that is the doctrine of error, which has held the whole world hostage with false gospel, has been revealed and we are witnesses to this TRUTH. Therefore believe the gospel and act now according to the revelation in Acts 2 verse 38 and 39.

All that you need to ask yourself is, "where do I belong?" If you are a Jew, congratulations; a child of an Israelite, that is okay; even if you are a Gentile, it does not matter; for the same gospel for the Jew is also for the Gentiles." Acts 2:39 The same doctrine will also work for you only if you believe. But you cannot be able to come to the true knowledge of this if God has not ordained you. Rom. 8:29, 30.

If you will not believe the WORD of God unto being baptized in water, you will not be able to receive the cleansing of your conscience that would purge and wash you away from the dirt of your hereditary and personal offenses. Consider 1 Pet. 3:21, 22.

The Pharisees and lawyers trusting on their own wisdom did not consider the baptism in water appropriate and so their hearts remained darkened. Luke 7:30. It is through baptism in water, in the name of Jesus Christ that a person could be clothed with Christ and have his name written in the book of life. Gal. 3:27. Anyone who have not received the forgiveness of sins though may be devoted and committed like Cornelius yet, he lacks. It is when a person has been purified through the machinery in forgiveness of sins that he can be worthy to enter into everlasting life having been made pure before God. Rev. 21:27.

CHAPTER 7

THE EVIDENCE OF TRUE SALVATION

In concluding this expository study about the irrevocable Bible standard of the doctrine of Salvation: I will like to look into another very important aspect of Salvation as it relates to mankind. Human obedience to the commandment of God does nothing to affect the glory of God; rather, all is for the total good of the man. The true church however, is the Kingdom of Christ Jesus designed as an instrument of warfare against the kingdom of darkness and these two kingdoms are presently at war. Eph. 6:12. To be equipped in this spiritual battle each and every believer must receive some particular spiritual weapons, which the individual must be a specialist in operating. Whatever that God has given you as long as you are in the Body has been made available to you in order to assist you in this battle and you must use your gift/s in a very credible manner because a time is coming, we will give account of these resources. 1 Cor. 12:4-11. Can we understand this simple fact, that there is power and also mighty power, if not for anything, we should believe that God is able to do all things through the things around us? Your knowledge, material resources and every singular thing around you can be overcharged with power from God and made strong in helping you defeat the evil forces; that is the reason why that in many circumstances where God would perform a miracle He does it by utilizing the available to create the needed. Ex. 4:1- 4, Mark 6: 38. Imagine the Israelites of old being confronted from behind by the terror of merciless Egyptian army and in front of them the sea stood as a barrier wall of impossibility and all that the Israelites could do was to weep and cry hopelessly. In that circumstance what the LORD empowered was the ordinary rod in the hand of Moses because faith was found in non-other Israelite than Moses and the sea was parted. Have you ever imagined what could have happened if there were more men of faith who stood their ground with Moses or where the entire people instead of reproofing God and blaming Moses burst into singing and rejoicing of faith, in fact, God could have unleashed several powers imbedded in more than just the rod? The unbelief of the people limited God to the rod of Moses. An ounce of Uranium is all that is needed to build strong atomic bomb which has the ability of destroying and devastating wide areas but I tell you that God has embedded more energy and power on non-radioactive substances and where we operate with faith these would be triggered against the kingdom of darkness and the devil can never stand the destruction machine.

That the church of God is able to move forward without the kingdom of darkness stopping it is because of the availability of spiritual weapons and their good use, so you can get the idea how the LORD will look on any who hid his/her gift selfishly to his/herself – the offense amount to sabotage of the Kingdom. Matthew 16 verse18, compare with Matthew 25 verse 34 to 46.

How can a person who has been born into the family of God receive some of these gifts as to be prepared for war? At any rate, we have no other to look unto but Christ Jesus, whom we must emulate and in questions like this, we need not to worry but to ask the FATHER through our Lord Jesus Christ what our heart desires are and because it is very important to us, we need to persist in our prayers until we receive answers. Heb. 12:2. But I must say this very quickly that our gifts are already with us all we need to do is to pray that God would open our eyes so that we can be able to identify them. Your gift in the Kingdom race include those areas you perform very well and the resources you already have been blessed with. Apart from the things around us which are given to us by God of which we must make adequate use of there is one particular gift that is not around us which we must crave for and plead with God until we have received it because without it, we cannot be able to journey through the strait and narrow path into the KINGDOM of GOD – it is non other than the gift of PROPHEY. 1 Cor. 14: 1, 5. This gift ought to be received and awaken at the time a person receives the Holy Spirit but where it is not experienced, there is the need to desire for it through fasting and prayers. Any moment a person is filled with the Holy Spirit, the gift of prophesy is undoubtedly the manifestation of such infilling and when it is not there we must do all we can to make sure it is there because it assures our faith.

To really prove to the whole world that he is the Messiah, the Christ of God, our LORD fasted to acquire ALL the spiritual gifts necessary to bring the Ministry of salvation to the reach of all creation. John 3:34. Since Jesus Christ, was the only one who came from heaven and the life in the spirit, no man knows about therefore, it was absolutely necessary that all the ways and manners of life in the spirit will have to be exemplified by our Lord. Our LORD to satisfy the conditions of discovering and acquiring ALL and EVERY spiritual gifts used the forty days and forty nights fasting and praying. Mark 1:12, 13.

It took our Lord Jesus Christ forty days and forty nights to be able to acquire and manifest in the full ALL the spiritual gifts. Coming to us, the gifts of the Spirit cannot come full and manifest completely upon a single individual but one must receive at least one of these gifts, which he will use to be profitable to the church. It is awful for any other man to attempt fasting for forty days like our Lord in order to awaken the Spirit. Three days of fasting and praying is ideal and commendable however, the length of one's fasting does not really matter; what matters most is how prepared is the inner man. On the other hand, it is possible for a man to truly identify his/her spiritual gifts without seeking them through fasting or food abstinence – there is another fasting the LORD appreciates. When you go to work for a week and devote your pay packet for that period to the poor, widows, fatherless and the Ministry or even when you sell some of your properties to upgrade the life of the less privileged; you are recognized before God more than that man who has gone without food and water for days, who know not mercy. Is. 58: 5 - 7. Instead of a hunger strike and be condemned before God, it is better you fill your bowel, have strength to do work which will benefit you and your neighbor and God would approve your sacrifice.

Some fasting could run for many days when it is not done day and night like our LORD'S. Fasting could also come by some personal denial of pleasure for the upgrading of the spirit for some long time. Dan. 10:2, 3.

When someone has identified his gift through fasting and prayer, the same is also needed from time to time to keep the fire burning through the same process. If there is weakness in your area of vocation, it takes fasting and praying to be awakened and alive again.

POINTS TO REMEMBER!

1. The conviction to be baptized into the Father, Son and Holy Spirit comes by the preaching of the good news; which is Christ Jesus revealed. Luke 24:46, 47.

2. John, the Baptist, physically demonstrated baptism into the Father. Acts 19:4. Baptism into the Father as it affects the church come by God through the preaching of the gospel and not in water or in other materials. 1 John 5:1, Eph. 5:26.

3. Baptism into the Son is the only baptism done in water as a symbol of burying by totally dipping the man into water. It is wrong and unscriptural to perform the baptism into the Son with the compound name Father, Son and Holy Spirit because neither FATHER nor the HOLY SPIRIT tested the corruption of dieing. Even when our LORD was about to give up ghost, both the FATHER and the HOLY SPIRIT deserted him according to Mark 15 verse 34. So it was Jesus Christ alone that died on the cross and only into the living tomb of our LORD can any man be buried and also rise again. The Bible injunction of Matthew 28 verse 19 is a compressed summary of all the baptisms needed by sinful man in order to obtain

93

everlasting life. When it comes to water baptism, it must be, only in the name of Jesus Christ.

4. A person is thrown into water for the baptism into Christ Jesus only one time. Water baptism in the name of Jesus Christ cannot be done twice in a lifetime, neither can a person be thrown and risen from water more than once. However, a person can experience several demonstrational claims about baptism in water many times but in as much as the baptism he now is upholding does not correspond with the Bible water baptism, that has the promise of salvation, such must be rightly re-baptized. Acts 19:3-5.

5. Baptism in the water is only in the name of Jesus Christ. The effectiveness of this baptism boarder only within the true church. The observation of this baptism without the upholding of the wholesome doctrine, faith and teachings of the truth makes such of no effect. Whenever there is a spiritual exercise there is always a probing into the personalities involved therefore we all must be careful of deceivers and impostors. Acts 19:13-16. A person could be baptized several times into the name of Jesus Christ in water as long as such baptisms were done by organizations or person/s that has not the wholesome doctrine, faith, beliefs and teachings of our Lord Jesus Christ. The moment such person comes to the truth he will be certainly re-baptized into the, *'one baptism.'* 'Eph. 4:5.

6. To be baptized means to dip, therefore baptism means the principle of dipping into. Baptism into water cannot be the same as sprinkling with water but to dip into water. If John, in water, baptized Christ Jesus and our LORD also got other people baptized in water through His disciples, it is wrong for anyone to practice sprinkling of water as to mean the same thing. John 3:22, 23.

94

7. Baptism in any way is not a child's affair! Baptism is for those who are physically and mentally mature, who can consciously access the word of God and discern the truth unto believing. The concept/tradition of baptizing infants is totally outside of the scripture, man-made and a false doctrine of the devil. An infant or a minor cannot be able to satisfy the condition for right baptism. Rom. 10:9. (Compare with Acts 8:36 and Rom. 10:10). God is very orderly and have consideration for all mankind including the infants and minors. According to the doctrine, the infant and minors remain under the physical as well as spiritual guidance and protection of the parent/s until maturity is reached. 1 Cor. 7:14.

8. A sinner who has been pre-ordained to eternal life will receive the gift of Repentance from God with which his stony heart is made flesh – this is the Touching of God. The very moment a person is touched by God, which is what is meant by receiving the gift of Repentance, at that point, he is made ready to be baptized in water. Baptismal Class, ceremonial arrangements and occasional preparations are not only unscriptural but work contrary to the truth. On the day of Pentecost, three thousand people were baptized immediately they got repented. Acts 2:40, 41. The Ethiopian eunuch who knew not Philip in time past encountered the gospel unprepared, yet reaching a body of water, Philip baptized him. Acts 8:36-39. The jailor received his baptism at nighttime and so on. Never was there any Bible record of baptismal classes, occasional preparation or ceremonial arrangements for baptism.

9. Baptism in water is a ritual initiation into the one body of Christ Jesus and one Family fellowshipping. Though the Bible did not say whether the Ethiopian eunuch later went to fellowship with brethren, however, judging by God's unchanging standard that after initiation, the

new convert must be taught and groomed in the word and instructions of Christ Jesus. Matt. 28:20. On the other hand, since the Ministry and establishment of the households of God are to reach out to people and places therefore, it may not be far from the truth that the church was extended to Ethiopia through the eunuch. Acts 1:8.

10. It is true that the Holy Spirit is given at the laying on of hands of the apostle according to Simon's observation in Acts 8 verse 18 yet, we are all aware that the Holy Spirit belongs solely to God and not the apostles' or prophets'. It is to promote unity and ensure inter-dependency of ministerial networks that God made this to be so. However, at extra-ordinary times like the day of Pentecost, the Holy Spirit came directly from God unto the church placing every other man second-ary and irrelevant. Coming to the house of Cornelius, the Omnipotent and Omniscience God knew that it was impossible for the Jews to impart the Holy Spirit upon (Cornelius) a Gentile. Therefore, God also sent down the Holy Spirit upon Cornelius and his household to the surprising of the Jewish believer. Even more, when it was impossible for Peter and the rest of the original apostles to recognize the repentance of Saul, the former persecutor, whom God changed to Paul; and whereas God places His Ministry above man and his pride, therefore, and again, a man who was not known to be an apostle, who may have been a prophet by calling did the work Peter could have done. Acts 9:17-19. It suf-fices therefore to say that at times when there is peace and quietness in the land and the church is moving on with the entire fivefold ministry in operation there should not be any schism; rather, the workload of the Ministry will have to be divided accordingly with the apostles charged with the exclusive duty of laying on of hands for the receiving of the Holy Spirit. Where there

is war, persecution or some other disturbances that endangers co-operation and availability, God can impart the Holy Spirit into a new believer through the laying on of hands of another who may not be an apostle.

11. The Doctrine of Salvation as enumerated in this book has been designed by God to bringing us to the true loving purpose of God! However, the ritual aspect of the doctrine will at a time expire along side with every prophecy, speaking in tongues and so on. 1 Cor. 13:8-10, 13. Where the knowledge of this doctrine does not bring you into the practice of true love towards God and your neighbor; you stand condemned already and cannot enter into the Kingdom of God. 1 John 2:9-11, 4:6-8.

May I warn here that the church must not deal with the things of God with contempt: the laying on of hands for the receiving of the Holy Spirit is not the business of elders or deacons but boarder between the apostles and prophets! Eph. 2: 20. The church has never been built upon the elders and deacons; rather history has it that these two has been the organizers of problems for the church from the wilderness even unto the covenant of new in Christ Jesus. Paul will not leave the church in the hands of the elders without regrets, because as a prophet he saw what would happen when he will be gone. Acts 20: 29, 30. Apostle however is a compound word and comprises of the joint calling of evangelists, pastors, teachers and prophets. Commissioning of workers must not be confused with this sensitive task that could be dated back to the Old Testament. Never did any elder in Israel of old officiate in the ordination of kings and priests, rather, only the High Priest or the Prophet of Jehovah God could. Those elders that thought of equating themselves with Moses and Aaron, God never took lightly with. Num. 16:1-3, 19-34.

SECTION B

TESTIMONY FROM THE AUTHOR

My name is Noah Chibuike Orji; I am the second to the youngest sons of late Pastor Johnson W. Orji and Nkasi Dorothy Orji (nee Obomanu). The whole family knows and calls me Chiboy, even after I am grown and become a man.

About the year 1987, my father, Pastor Johnson Wugochukwu Orji was one day with me when the LORD sent one man from Calabar, Nigeria, to warn my father, he said, "The Lord visited me and commanded me to go to Pastor Orji and warn him because he is over relaxing and not doing the work of God; and behold souls are perishing into hell fire." My father and I were filled with surprise as the man went on, "The Lord also told me to tell Pastor Orji that if he will not rise up from his sleep and do the work, He (GOD) will visit Pastor Orji's house with a punishment ears will hear and tingle." The man admitted that his denomination (Faith Tabernacle Congregation) does not believe in prophecy but since the Lord God had visited him severally in the dream with express massage he had no choice than to comply. Pastor Orji humbly replied, "I don't doubt prophecy, however I am now in my nineties; I have dim eyes; my bones and arteries are weak by age and all my manliness has gone away from me and now I am waiting here because I know I will soon return to where I came from. While I was young, I did the much I could and I gave the totality of my strength to the service of God and in me I am satisfied that I have labored. That the Lord is requiring me again to rise and work in this my condition, I cannot tell, why? However, I will summon more courage and see what more I can do." The man went on to say, "God had spoken to me two times to go to Pastor Orji and deliver this message but I defaulted. The third time, the Lord, warned me, 'If you would not go as you have been commanded, you will receive greater punishment than that I will visit Pastor Orji with.'" He also said that when he inquired of the Lord, where to find Pastor Orji, the same Lord told him, 'Pastor Orji has since retired to his village; to get to his village you need to stop first at Aba Motor Park, ask for those going to Ezinihite Mbaise, stop at Obizi and take a motor bike to Umuofo Udo, there inquire for Pastor Orji's residence.'

At first I thought the man was cracking some jokes but when I realize how furious he was I knew something was really the matter, but I was yet to find out as the man went on again to say, "While I was in the dream, I saw the LORD bring before Pastor Orji: Eternity zinc, Iron beams, Gravels, Sand, Cement and powerful Nails; all these were heaped in one corner. On the other side was also loaded: Mats, Bamboo sticks, Raffia robes and Mud. A voice came to Pastor Orji, saying, 'Choose either of these and build your house!'"

With all these I became deeply worried and thoughts cumbered me, how come about that the man would talk to my father like this, seeing his condition of health and who can he be referring to as the LORD; could it be me that the he is referring to, indirectly. 'What a coincidence that the man could come when everyone had gone out leaving only myself and my father.' Thoughts flooded my mind! Later on, God made me to know that HE used that meeting to transfer the anointing of my father to me like it happened with Elijah and Elisha.

The man also recalled when he was converted to Faith Tabernacle Congregation sometime in the early forties; how he came into the faith with the dreaded disease gonorrhea, but was perfectly healed after Pastor Orji, my father, prayed for him. He also witnessed how he was physically present when Pastor Orji prayed and raised the dead and since then he knew that God was with Pastor Orji.

The man did not salute or shake hands with my father when he came in to our house but simply asked, "I am looking for the house of Pastor Orji", "I am Pastor Orji and this is my house, you may come in and have a seat." My father politely replied. According to the man, not shaking hands with Pastor Orji the very time he came in was in response to the separation between my father and his denomination, since according to the dogma of Faith Tabernacle Congregation members are restricted to shake hands with those that are no more fellowshipping with them. After the man delivered the message that he received from God and having confirmed that my father was an elect of God according to what has been shown to him in revelation, the man then shook hands with my father and embraced him and said, "I can not condemn whom the LORD has justified."

According to my father, in 1945, there was a very serious power tussle in Faith Tabernacle Congregation, Nigeria. Pastor Orji, my father, was made Pastor and General Manager of schools of the whole Faith Tabernacle Congregation in 1929 in Nigeria. Unlike very many of the pastors in those days that were not lettered, my father was advantaged with Standard Six Certificate. Many of the educationally disadvantaged pastoral colleagues of my father became jealous of him, conspired against him and paid an assassin hundred pounds to kill him but God would not allow them; and when every effort made to kill my father failed, Joshua, a six-year old boy and the first son of my father was murdered in cold blood. Not only that the conspirators murdered my stepbrother, Joshua, in a cold blood but they also went further to influence justice in the court of law that the suspects were discharged and acquitted for want of evidence. Consequently, my father, Pastor Johnson Wugochukwu was accused to have killed his own son, Joshua, which led to an enquiry from the church Headquarters in Philadelphia. My father after sending his memorandum of defense to the church Headquarters; Nigeria was advised to re-instate my father but his colleagues will not accept.

May all glory, honor, adoration and thanks be ascribed unto God and God alone: who is the avenger of His elect, for all that heard and concealed; saw but never told how the innocent boy was murdered, were judged by God, each dieing mysteriously and at the same time, confessed!

I was still in the loins of my father in those days; no one had ever thought about my mother at that time, much less about me but God knew me even from the foundation of the world and maybe, the devil was somehow suspicious that something great would come out of earthen vessel, for which reason he sought to destroy my father. The first wife of my father died in the late forties and later he took another wife, my mother, in 1955, Nkasi Dorothy Orji (nee Obomanu).

102

Few years after I was born, in 1963, Nigerian civil war broke out and the devil again targeted to destroy me like he did to my stepbrother, Joshua. My mother will never forget the incident that could have taken away my life, she tearfully said to me, "I can never forget that day when you fell sleep and I lay you down on a mat and went to take a shower; from the bathroom I heard a terrible sound and hurriedly I came out, lo and behold Nigerian artillery pieces had busted the roof and fell right beside where you were laid. You were crying and I took you to myself and knew nothing could have saved your life than the Almighty God. From that time I realized that your life would be to the glory of God who saved you for a purpose I was yet to know." My mother concluded!

I so much thank God for my parents who never despised prophecy.

While the whole family was resident in the Northern region of Nigeria and being of Ibo origin the Lord Jesus Christ came and revealed the terror of the civil war to my mother. By the revelation of our LORD and obedience to act timely, our family was save from the gruesome civil war in Nigeria at that time. Many people of Ibo origin were massacred in the Northern Region of Nigeria: several Ibo women were raped to death; pregnant women cut through with knives and their young ones dashed to the stone; young men thrown into the River Niger and many were brutally murdered. Since the family knows that God still speaks today, and though my mother was still with Faith Tabernacle Congregation, yet she believed God and left Kafanchan, Plateau State, Nigeria. Just after we had crossed safely into the Eastern Nigeria, home of the Ibos, we began to hear news of how the Ibos living in the Northern Region were brutally murdered exactly as it was revealed.

About the year 1975 my parents bought the family

house at 17 Adimoha Street, off Obohia Road, Aba, Abia State, Nigeria. My father, Pastor Johnson Wugochukwu had his will written, instructing his children to have equal rights to his property and that no member of his family should cheat on another.

Sometime in the late eighties, Emmanuel I. Orji, the first son of my parents   went and told our father that he would like him to release to him the documents of the family house because he wanted to use them to obtain loan from the bank so that he could execute some contract jobs he worn from NAFCON. Emmanuel also promised to be giving our father some percentage of the profit which he would make from the jobs he would be doing in NAFCON, and because of the financial benefit expected by our father and pressure from our mother, he consented and surrendered the house documents to his son, outside the knowledge of the rest of us.

Several years passed bye, my father did not receive a penny from the son neither did he return the house documents and when our father sensed danger and became very much worried, he sent for me and told me all that had gone on between him and my older brother. "You have not done well," I told my father, "You should realize that the property does not belong to you anymore, since you have gotten a lot of sons and a daughter and it is against the God you serve and the will you have made; for you to give your property to a particular child of yours or some particular children." 'What can I do now to correct the error that I have done?' My father asked, humbly! "Call an emergency meeting of all your family members and make this issue known; apologize to all of us and see the response." I suggested!

A family meeting was quickly arranged and in that meeting Emmanuel was mandated by the family to return the house documents as soon as possible. Days, months and years passed but the house documents were not returned and later we received a report that some money were still owed to the lending firm and that was the reason why we could not get the house papers back.

Our in-law, Chief Nzenwa, brought the thirty five thousand naira needed to pay the creditors, VALUELINE so that they would release our family house documents. Emma went with Elijah my immediate senior brother and paid the money to VALUELINE and obtained a receipt instructing them to come on a later date and collect the papers. The next story was that the documents could not be found because some unscrupulous elements working with the financial company may have stolen them.

Every effort made to see that these lost documents were realized was dramatically blocked and in the midst of all these my father called me and said, 'I have seen that there is some foul play on the family house documents which I gave to your brother, you are the only one that I know that can remedy this situation and find my house documents and you must do so fast now that I am still alive because if I am gone you may have so much trouble with your brothers because I know you stand for the truth therefore, find a way to get back the family house documents before it becomes too late.' My father tearfully said.

After consulting with a lawyer, Barrister Chibundu (late), on behalf of my father, a certified true copy of the missing document was obtained from the Ministry of Lands; my father also got an affidavit of loss of deed; and coupled with other official protocols, the missing house document were declared null and void. According to the instructions of the attorney that the situation necessitated that an entirely different document needed to be raised to be able to contend with the articles in the first therefore, an irrevocable power of attorney over the family house was given to me by my father with an instruction that I must make sure the property is well protected and every person's right preserved.

The health of my mother, Nkasi Dorothy Orji, started going down badly that one of my senior brothers, Hezekiah U. Orji (Zeke) returned from the US and took her with him to the United States of America where she received treatment and become completely well; our father left the village shortly thereafter and joined us (myself, Elijah and Ezekiel) at 17 Adimoha Street, Aba.

All his life and much more this time, when sickness and age have become unfriendly, my father, Pastor Johnson Wugochukwu, a man of God, was always making a particular prayer, time and time again: "My God and my Father, please have mercy on me and show me the way that I have not done well before you, that I may amend my ways; and no matter what, let your grace bring me into your holy presence, where I will abide forever. This I pray in the Mighty name of Jesus Christ. Amen!"

My father read through the Bible, sixty-six times: from Genesis to Malachi and from Matthew to Revelation; word for word and line for line, without lenses and when he could no longer see, God empowered him with a strong memory that on his sick bed he kept reciting several key verses of the scriptures like, Isaiah 40 verse 31, Matthew. 11:28-30 and so on. This habit and method of bible reading I got from my father and frankly speaking it has helped me so much in actualizing my ministry in a very unique way.

After I had received the message of the truth and accepted unto baptism in water in the name of Jesus Christ and became a preacher of the message, I used to share the word of God with my father and on one particular occasion when I talked about SALVATION, I said, "The true salvation of God in Christ Jesus can never be gotten except a person obey the word as to be baptized in the water and in the name of Jesus Christ. It is through this baptism that a person's name is written in the lamb's book of life and there can never be two baptisms." I emphasized, quoting and reading several scriptures to buttress my point, my father was so excited and exclaimed, "I have read the Bible these sixty-six times but I never understood what I read to this point, my son, maybe this is the answer for my age long prayer that God may show me the ways that I went wrong so I can really get myself ready to depart. I doubt not the scripture and though I have received baptism in the name of the Father, Son and Holy Ghost, I now see the difference and I believe and accept to be re-baptized in the name of Jesus Christ." According to the tender mercies of the Lord, my father accepted the ministration and was baptized in water, in the name of Jesus Christ. As we honor and glorify God who enabled this great miracle of salvation, we will never forget to appreciate the spiritual instructors whom God used in this service like, Remigius Uwaeme and Nnamdi Alozie (apostles of Jesus Christ). My special appreciation goes to one brother Oke (Mercedes), who volunteered his time and Mercedes car to take my father to the river where he was baptized.

The LORD came and told my father, Johnson Wugochukwu, "since you have been diligent to follow ME and have obeyed the principles in the doctrine of truth therefore, I, the MOST HIGH has granted you your desire to enter into MY KINGDOM and as an addition you shall not die until you have seen and also entered the kingdom of the world today." The LORD also made my father to realize that the United States of America is the visible kingdom of today's world. Sicknesses could not distort this vision and that it might be fulfilled that which was spoken by GOD; my father was later flown to the United States of America for treatment. By the time my father came into United States, the LORD opened his eyes and he not only saw the kingdom of the world today but he also entered into it according to the promises of GOD. My brother, Hezekiah, was expecting the same miracle of healing as was seen on our mother Dorothy; so, for more than four months, a team of doctors were attending to Pastor Johnson Wugochukwu but the condition was not within the corridors of orthodox medicine because the LORD would want HIS servant to come home and rest. My father, Pastor Johnson Wugochukwu later slept in the LORD, in the United States of America while staying in the house of his son, Hezekiah U. Orji (Zeke). Zeke brought home the body of our father and he was given a befitting burial.

After my father slept in the LORD, I saw in a dream at night, something that appeared like a computer but very big and while my father was departing in very smart attire like the Cowboys, the computer scrolled out and I witnessed that it was written there on the machine, 'Johnson Wugochukwu, a SAINT.'

At this point I would want to very quickly say that every word of God is true and can never be void and when the LORD is making strong statements, men ought to fear. However, if our eyes were to be opened, we would regret to realize that more than 95% of those confessing Christ, who pass into the great beyond, end up in hell fire? It is not easy to save one single soul and bring such into the kingdom of GOD and already the judgment has started from us who believe and will end with the world on the last day. So be very careful with your life and faith because God is watching you and certainly will bring you into judgment but pray let it be now and not later. 1 Peter 4:17, 18.

A person who has not the genuine Holy Spirit of God is blind in the spirit not knowing where he is coming from, the place he is standing now or where he is going. When such eventually dies, admirers may witness for him as having lived life worthy of emulation but right there in the home of the lost, he languishes. This is the more reason why each and every one of us must be very careful with our faith according to the warning of our LORD in Mark 13 verse 5.

After the death of my father, the devil again saw another opportunity to attempt on my life!

The burial went as was planned, our mother Nkasi Dorothy stayed for some time and her health began again to deteriorate that she had to arrange going back to the United States of America for medical attention. When I saw what could possibly happen in the future I suggested to our mother to make sure she shared the rooms in the family house among the members of the family according to the instructions of our late father before she would go back to the United States of America. Every member of our family accepted the move with the exception of Emmanuel, who also was the only one absent on the day the family came together for the sharing. Notwithstanding the absence of Emmanuel, the rest family went on and shared the property and communicated officially to all concerned on the resolutions.

When it was realized that the property's documents had been updated and the missing documents annulled, there were conspiracies that led to the assassination attempt on my life by my three brothers - Emmanuel, Elijah and Onyekwere. The three came suddenly on me just as I was coming out from the bathroom with only my towel rapped across my waist. "What have you done?" Emmanuel demanded! Before I could reply to the question, all the three brothers started raining blows on me. I was stripped of my towel and made completely naked. My wife, Basilia Uchechukwu, saw how my three brothers were seriously beating me, and interrupted by saying, "You will kill your brother, please I beg you leave him," Emmanuel turned towards my wife with his iron rod and hit a three months pregnant woman on her forehead. Basilia had to climb and jump over a burglary protector and though she disjointed her ankle, yet she remains thankful to God for saving her life that day.

I struggled with my three brothers and when I saw that it had come to a question of life and death, I grabbed Emmanuel and gave him a big bite on the chest, holding on until the man became weak, ceasing that opportunity I tried to escape but Ezekiel grabbed me by my neck and hit my head against the wall; stars came out of my eyes but the LORD was with me that I did not fall but ran away for my dear life, completely naked.

For the love and confidence I have for my only sister Chioma, who is married and lives with the husband in the town, I ran to Umungasi to tell her what had happened. I was still speaking to my sister in her room when the husband came in and interrupted, inviting me to his sitting room. "What were you discussing with your sister", Chief Christian Nzenwa asked, "I was just telling her how my brothers came and attempted to murder me" I replied. "I can not believe that my own brothers would for any reason whatsoever attempt on my life like they did today, I am really disappointed." I lamented. To my greatest surprise my in-law, replied, "I was the one who sent your brothers to come and murder you, I told them to make sure you are beaten until you have lost consciousness then they can take you to the nearby hospital where you will be treated; if you survive, I instructed them to use the police force and arrest you, take you from the hospital and straight to police custody; there you will be tortured until you accept to give me the land documents." On hearing this, I was frozen; I thought it was a dream; I started praying within my soul. While the Chief was yet speaking, the phone rang, he quickly picked it, "It is your brother, Elijah who has just called and he said he will be here soon," the Chief thundered! "I told him that you are

110

here." Shortly, the phone rang again and he picked it again and said to me in great disgust, "Your brother Emma has just called and told me that he is also coming; you have no choice now than to submit to him or you will die; I have chosen to sponsor them to any length to make sure they deal with you." The Chief decreed, like a god! The God of Abraham, Isaac and Jacob and the merciful Father of Pastor Johnson Wugochukwu was the only one that can save me from this danger that I walked into! I sat down and soon afterwards my brother Elijah came in; I thought, 'This maybe my last fight for life.' I encouraged myself and was ready to use my last strength to the glory of God. I never can tell how God saved me that day but all I know was that: God sent his angels who came down and blinded the eyes of them all so that I could escape. From there I ran to the house of my stepbrother, Samuel Ndubuisi Orji and narrated my ordeal to him.

From that moment I became unusually alert and to trust any close relative became a problem to me. That evening I was visited by my wife Basilia, who now was wearing bandage on her disjointed ankle, for she had earlier ran to her father's house at 8 Nwosu Street, Aba, with our children. Basilia, an orphan, notwithstanding her condition and pains had to trace me, her husband, to 49 Okwu Avenue where I went on exile and while we were reflecting on our traumatic moments, I also told my wife how I again escaped another death trap in Umungasi, when I went to complain to my sister. "Did I hear you say you went to your sister, Da Chioma, in Umungasi? Did you not know that she came with your three brothers and was shouting on top of her voice and cursing us and when she saw that I had already escaped to the yard of Anayo Ereh, she demanded, 'Come here you foolish woman and die with your husband; you want to be a landlady; why then are you running?'" My wife spoke tearfully with every amount of disgust. "God really loves you, I must confess but you don't have to play with your life and I am not ready to be a widow in my youth: you just have to be careful, if not for my sake, just think about your little children." Basilia pleaded from a wounded heart! I was speechless for minutes: my mind went out from me and I was confused, 'Maybe I have believed on my brothers and sister more than I should have and it would have been nice if I trusted in God than to put confidence in my relatives?' I pondered!

Early in the morning the next day, I was sitting at the parlor ponderous and looking out through the window, I saw my sister drive into the premises where I was staying in exile: I raised an alarm and quickly ran into one of the toilet apartment and hide myself. My sister climbed the staircase and walked in but couldn't find me, and when they noticed I was hiding in the toilet for fear of death my stepbrother and my sister came and was asking me to come out from the toilet. From my hideout I cried and shouted, "I didn't know that Da Chioma, my sister will consent to the arrangement to murder me, I am not surprised so much that Chief Nzenwa would scheme for a way to eliminate me because he hated me from the first day he set his eyes on me. But what on earth would make my sister, Da Chioma to consider killing me; the sister I have cherished and loved like my own mother; if Da Chioma would rise up against me to shed my blood, O LORD how can I be another Caesar and my sister the Brutus?" I shouted and cried loud as I poured my mind in great sorrow and worst disappointment of life. My stepbrother, Samuel pleaded with me to come out from the toilet but I wouldn't, "Please go away from me, for I can see your hands stained with my blood, but my God said it will not be so." I mumbled out in sorrow! Though my sister, Chioma later denied that she was not present in the scene of the murder attempt on my life, yet, eyewitnesses confirmed her presence and her vehement expressions.

I was driven out from the family house with my

pregnant wife and two daughters and they ceased my personal belongings. When I saw there was no way out of the dilemma, I decided to go and stay with my in-laws at, No 8 Nwosu Street Aba and was there for four months. Elijah and Onyekwere quickly took over my only source of livelihood that was located there at No17 Adimoha St. Aba.

But my GOD did not let me alone but quickly came to my rescue and sent immediately one brother, by name, Obi, from Ebonyi State, Nigeria; the LORD used this young man immensely in keeping my family alive and well in those days of our troubles. Obi was a commercial motorcyclist in Aba as at then but when he saw my condition he was touched by God and as his custom had always been he decided rendering all his account money from his daily business to me. Obi assisted me to a tune of eighteen thousand and some fraction naira. Though I later paid Obi back his money, I will never forget such good gesture, "I still owe Obi and as the LORD lives by whom I stand it shall be well with him, and as my soul prospers so also shall Obi enjoy the fruit of his labor of LOVE."

The family house was later sold and every one of us had his inheritance! Shame went to the devil while Glory, honor and praise goes to our God.

Never receive the grace of GOD in vain!

One day, a man came to me in the dream and called me by the name, 'David' and I answered, "That is not my name, and I am Chibuike." The man went further to say, "You are David; you may not understand how for now but when the time shall come you will know."

Prophecies began coming in from the body of Christ and though they seem to be divided, some following Remigius Uwaeme and the other faction with Basil, yet the

113

two were bringing in messages that agree. A prophet from Enugu while we were having meeting in the house of one elder Benjamin in Umuimo, Nigeria said, "I saw where our brother, Chibuike, was coming back with lots of sheep tied with a rope one to another and one end of the rope was held by our brother, Chibuike, who was leading the sheep. There were very many sheep; some were black and others were white." I remember that on that same day the prophet also spoke as he was shown concerning another brother, Chuma, the evangelist, he said, "I saw where our brother Chuma, the evangelist, was carried up and placed on a kind of center table and a lot people were bringing accusations on him until he was lifted to a tree where one woman fed him with limited measure of food." In the side of Apostle Remigius Uwaeme several brethren witnessed prophetically concerning my ministry to the Western World, people like: Obinali, Earnest, Uche Dike, sister Erinma just to mention but a few.

It is true that the church in Nigeria commissioned me, as was Paul before I left for the United States according to the doctrine. It is also true that I did not demand for any assistance since the Lord Jesus Christ was using my biological family in the service. In the light of this however, there were no willing appreciations from brethren to the missionary work, which I was going in for which also the Holy Spirit had testified to, from the mouth of the prophets in the Body of Christ. I am convinced that God may have seen the need to take the gospel to the Western World and the nonchalant attitude of brethren that HE chose to do it this way to the exclusive glory of God. This is to me a strong proof that the scriptures are true and no man can stand against the plans of God in the expansion of the gospel, not even unloving brethren!

I had a very challenging experience when I came to the United State of America: I pleaded with my own brethren in Nigeria to assist the church but until this moment that I am writing this book, nothing has been done. When I had to talk to brother, Basil, who is also an apostle of Jesus Christ I was astonished when he told me that I should know that it was not the church that sent me to the United States and that I should therefore not look to them rather, I should find a way I can struggle it out. Elder Felix (Lovers Bread) only told me that I should realize that things are difficult in Nigeria and I should not expect them to send money to me from home. I believe that God saw all these and chose my senior brother, Hezekiah U. Orji (Zeke), who, even before his conversion, accommodated the church in his house and have been doing so much to help.

Maybe the reason why the LORD did not want me to be directly sponsored by either of the two factions is because the church must come to be united as one body. It was exclusively the ETERNAL FATHER in partnership with the SON JESUS CHRIST and by the efforts of my brother Hezekiah U. Orji (Zeke) that I was able to successfully enter the United States of America. Though the apostle of Jesus Christ, Basil and some of the elders, came together in Umuimo and commissioned me into the service of the Ministry like Paul, the same LORD hindered the brethren from demonstrating Christ LOVE toward me – not a single brother gave a dine for my travel. I believe that this was done that it might be fulfilled that which God does purpose because I was brought to the United States of America to defend the TRUTH without compromise or respect for any man or sect.

I remember when I entered the United States of America newly, I was with my brother, Hezekiah U. Orji, my mother, Dorothy Nkasi Orji, my nephews, Michael, Lionel and Edward; we were all in 3421 S 263rd St. Kent, Washington State before I later moved to my own house with my mother. 26826 Military Rd. S., Kent, Washington

State. I preached the gospel to the family and they believed, not only because the Word was strong and with quotable justifications from the Bible but much more because there were outbursts of prophecy and the demonstration of God's love and power.

God has really taken me from a very long way; protecting and preserving my life; maybe, for the purpose of spreading this gospel of truth to all creatures according to the commandment of God in Christ Jesus.

Never has this issue been taken lightly; this testimony is given that you might be strengthened. That God has been saving you from plane crash, motor accident and so on is not just a natural phenomenon, rather, it could be a divine program to preserve your life as to usher you into this knowledge of truth.

When I realized what God is doing, I became more and more alert to pick illumination from the Lord Jesus Christ and to put them down on paper. This book is one of my many books the LORD has helped me to put together so that you may read and meditate; comparing and contrasting with the scriptures and world events in the area of the gospel message.

Like Paul of old, I have met a lot of challenges in the race and the devil has been doing all he can to make sure he either abort my apostolic calling or exchange my inheritance. Glory is to God for a brother like Felix Eze (Chairman, Managing Director Lover Bread), Basil, (the apostle of Jesus Christ), Sam, Innocent and the indomitable brethren from Owerri. May the LORD keep and bless you all because you will not give in to the watering of the truth but you should look for the love of Christ Jesus when it is still day. Rev. 2:4.

Special thanks to my senior brother, Hezekiah U. Orji (Zeke): whom God is using immensely to bless my spirit; he was the one that filed petition on my behalf so I was granted immigrant visa into the United States of America. Zeke did not just stop at bringing me into the United States but also assisted me to be established. Zeke is a Doctor of Philosophy and the Chief Editor of my book.

To GOD be all the glory, honor, adoration and thanks for what HE has done to my father's house: just soon as I arrived the United States of America and preached this message of Salvation; my mother yielded and was baptized; then my brother Hezekiah and my nephew, Michael were also baptized to the glory of God. My mother became the first fruit in God's Salvation program to the United States and beyond.

In all, God has remained faithful to me!

The faithfulness of God endures forever, in the name of Jesus Christ.

Amen!

CONTACT:
The Author,
"PROMISED SAVED BUT ONLY DECEIVED"
26826 Military Rd. S.
Kent, WA. 980132,
United States of America.

Tel. 253-859-7957
E-mail - chibuikebasilia@yahoo.com

ISBN 141207767-2

9 781412 077675